SELF-REALIZATION
AND
SELF-DEFEAT

SELF-REALIZATION
AND
SELF-DEFEAT

Samuel J. Warner, Ph.D.

Grove Press, Inc.   New York

Whatever a hater may do to a hater, or an enemy to an enemy, a wrongly-directed mind will do us greater mischief.

Buddha

CONTENTS

PREFACE

Every human obviously wants to succeed—to realize the best of his potentials. And yet many of us clearly defeat ourselves in life.

This is a shocking paradox, and yet it is true: Some people are their own worst enemies; they consistently prepare traps into which they themselves fall.

It is not a question of intelligence. Self-defeatists are often extremely intelligent, but use only part of their brain power constructively. The remainder is used to undo what went before—to end a project with a crippling and over-all failure.

Furthermore, it is not a question of sanity. However much self-defeat insults man's conception of himself as a rational creature, we are forced to admit that self-defeatists are often encountered among those who are clearly rational and sane.

Then what *is* it a question of? Why and how do we defeat ourselves?

These are questions the answers to which I have been

seeking for the past fifteen years through clinical research. I have published several reports of my findings.

These reports have been for the professional, the specialist. I now want to reach the non-professional, the man who may himself be involved in some form of chronic self-defeat.

I want to share with you what I have learned about the "how" and "why" of self-defeat. I believe that what I have to say can be helpful to you in two major ways.

First: "Know thyself" is ancient wisdom. If one is alerted to the signs of self-defeat, one can better discover its pitfalls in one's personal life—and avoid them.

Second: There are times when self-help is not enough. I want to present a clear picture of how psychotherapy may help dissolve patterns of self-defeat, for one is more likely to employ a potentially useful "tool" if one understands the reasons for its usefulness.

So let us now proceed with our analysis of the forces which make for self-defeat, and of therapeutic procedures whereby one may be helped to free himself—to achieve a greater degree of self-realization. And we shall center our exploration upon the world within, believing with the gifted introspectionist Sören Kierkegaard—of man and his yearning—"so by turning inwardly he discovers freedom."

—S. J. W.

I

PATTERNS OF SELF-DEFEAT[1]

"Man is born free, and everywhere he is in chains," proclaimed Jean Jacques Rousseau midway in the eighteenth century. For although man was created a free agent, later experiences in society severely hampered his freedom for self-initiated creative behavior, and led to the curtailment and distortion of his actualized self.

Rousseau's concern was largely with social chains, with the customs and laws of society which hamper creative intelligence. Our concern is primarily with *inner* chains, with blocks within the human mind itself; with those functional chains—which are considerably more difficult to perceive or to comprehend with clarity—binding self-realization.

When people consider their failure to succeed in some aspect of life, they generally overlook completely the causal roles played by forces within themselves in the ultimate outcome of that failure. For people generally maintain a clever camouflage of "good" and situational reasons for such consistent failure, so as to direct the burden of blame away from themselves. The student finds the teacher inadequate; the artist blames the medium in which he works; the young executive finds office politics insurmountable—all point outward for the cause of their failure to achieve creative fulfillment.

Yet intensive study of the life situations of these people often reveals the more basic cause of failure to lie within the student, the artist, and the executive themselves. Analysis proves these people time and again to be subtly self-defeating.

But our insights into self-defeat are difficult to perceive and to comprehend. We all tend to believe that every living thing seeks only its own advantage in life. And it shocks our basic orientation to the living even to contemplate the possibility that some of us persistently and urgently seek our own *dis*-advantage. Therefore this problem of self-defeat has been termed a "great puzzle" and a "stumbling block to psychology and psychiatry."

Nevertheless, in the clinical situation, to which such self-defeating people come for help—wondering what sort of people they could be if they dissolved these blocks to creative living—in this special situation, with its special inner pressures toward honest perception, we have been fortunate enough in the past forty years or so to make considerable headway into the problem of self-defeat.

Let us devote a chapter to various patterns of self-defeat. In subsequent chapters we shall delve into the underlying causes of such hampered self-realization.

We begin with the clinical situation, for it was here that I first became aware of this most puzzling of paradoxes: that many people who appear at the clinic in ostensible search for help toward successful self-realization through psychotherapy prove upon investigation to be unquestionably engaged in defeating themselves in those very processes of psychotherapy. These people clearly wish to thwart the achievement of successful psychotherapy.

It was the dedicated psychoanalyst Karl Abraham who first called attention to these bewildering occurrences of self-defeat in the clinical situation. And it was to this puzzling phenomenon that Sigmund Freud applied the term "the negative therapeutic reaction." For, said Freud, such persons perversely grew worse in treatment at the very time when all signs pointed to a readiness for marked improvement. It was a "negative" reaction, for it took exactly the opposite direction from the therapeutic success Freud believed he had a right to expect.

Foremost psychoanalysts rushed to explain this slight to their therapeutic powers, and their writings [2] offer profound insights into the dynamics of self-defeat. Karen Horney has contributed signally to our knowledge of self-defeat in the clinical setting. She summed up the self-defeating patient's unconscious aim succinctly: "He will go to any length to defeat the analyst's efforts, even though in so doing he obviously defeats his own ends."

Insights into this phenomenon have been explicit for thousands of years. The Bible treats self-and-other defeat in a number of places,[3] as in the concept of Satan. And in post-Biblical literature, Goethe was one of many who wrote of Mephistopheles' wish for ultimate self-and-other destruction—that ". . . all that exists should be annihilated."

In philosophy, Nietzsche has contributed mightily to our understanding of self-defeat. His terms are crude, but his genius shines through an early statement of the problem: "I call an animal, a species, and an individual corrupt, when it loses its instincts, and selects and *prefers* that which is detrimental to it."

In psychoanalysis, the term "masochism" has been much used to denote such self-defeating tendencies. The term is derived from the Austrian novelist Leopold von Sacher-Masoch, who, in the latter half of the last century, described sexual aspects of this problem: the linkage of sexual pleasure with the receiving of cruel treatment.

There is a rapidly growing fund of clinical accounts of such self-hurt. But "masochism," as a term, has been used in so many different ways that it is by no means entirely analogous to our terms "self-defeat" and "lack of freedom to achieve." There are "erotogenic masochism," "ideal masochism," "moral masochism," "primary masochism," and others—all with varying defining dimensions for their respective concepts.

A common element, however, in all of these concepts is this: *The individual tends to do that which is injurious to himself.* He apparently finds satisfaction for a deep need in this way, and even though he may be unaware both of the nature of the need and of its satisfaction, he gives ample evidence of its existence. "You're asking for trouble!" is the insight one gifted but self-defeating artist [4] came to perceive about herself as she became sufficiently free to recognize what was really taking place in her life. Another saw how truly effective he was in assisting other people to direct their lives—while he was incredibly inept in the management of his own. A third worked industriously and effectively to obtain desirable employment—only to have himself fired over flagrant indiscretions. A fourth went to the extreme of climbing tall chimneys while intoxicated, and then standing at their very edge—so that a misstep would mean severe pain and death.

Such people often suffer terribly at the hands of their self-defeating tendencies. The humiliations and quiet agonies engendered by work inhibitions and other facets of curtailed achievement often constitute nothing less than ordeals. They often suffer depression when they seek to create, and report these feelings as "fatigue." The Biblical expression "bricks without straw" well describes the pathetic image of the person who seeks to achieve successfully, and yet becomes depressed and seriously lacking in available energy at the moment when he seeks to act creatively. Further, there is often a need to suffer. Such a person seizes upon virtually every opportunity there is to achieve a state in which he will be miserable. Finally, and baffling though it may seem, at the very moment that the self-defeatist is wretched, when he is suffering the humiliation and torment of some misfortune, if you look into his eyes, their expression often betrays feelings of triumph and mockery! At the very moment that he complains bitterly of the crippling blows of fate, of severe frustration (and consequent personality disfigurement), he may well display a faint mocking smile. This, then, is often the pattern: they inwardly rejoice over self-hurt; they obviously find satisfaction in experiences which are punishing and self-destructive; yet they can feel "suffering" at the same time!

The foregoing may offend the good sense and rationality of the reader. He may feel this too outrageous to be true. Yet I shall endeavor to show in later chapters the many underlying forces sufficient to explain such strange behavior.

These people are clearly not free to achieve successfully, to employ their creative intelligence in order to improve their lot, to better their life for themselves. One bright and gifted young man, who had come gradually to perceive his inner need to suffer, said pathetically: "Why can't I just enjoy doing something *for* myself?" Another saw it in this light: "When I look back, I see how I haven't been looking out for myself—in the jobs I have taken." A third, who had repeatedly wasted opportunities for advancement phrased it this way: "I put a wall up before my-

self—to keep myself from going where I *really* want to go."
A brilliant scholar who was about to have a free summer
for the first time in years, listed the various things he was
going to do with his time. Upon reflection, it came as a
shocking surprise to him that all of these planned activities
constituted essentially a piddling away of his time—whereas
he had hungered for years to complete a creative project.
Apparently, the hunger to create is not enough: One must
in addition be inwardly free to pursue the creative task to
completion.

These self-defeatists become, so to speak, gargoyles of
their genotype. Their basic capacities dwarf their achievements. One young executive viewed his problem this way:
"I want to be able to *function*. I want to do my work the
way I somehow know that I *can* do my work." This young
man obviously possessed marked gifts and the potential for
successful productivity. Yet he had thus far realized—
what is so often encountered in our time—little more than
a complicated neurosis. His work history clearly demonstrated the perverse inclination away from a development
of his capabilities, and toward resounding self-defeat. He
consistently chose the "wrong" kind of job for himself; for
one reason or another, he gravitated toward work he despised, and which utilized his talents only minimally. Once
employed, he would, characteristically, energetically apply
himself for a short while, then lapse into passive-resistive
behavior made manifest in late-coming and procrastination,
which would eventually lead to his being fired. This pattern would be repeated time and again, and with the passing of years, it appeared likely that his entire life would be
engulfed in this personality quagmire.

Self-defeatists often manifest marked immaturity and
dependency. In presenting themselves to the world as in-
capable of assuming adult responsibilities, they maintain a

neurotic façade which permits them to avoid really coming to grips with the inherent issues of adulthood and mature creativity. Through such apparent immaturity and dependence, they thwart those who depend upon them. One passive-agressive man recalled: "When I was angry with my wife, I wouldn't work—to spite her." The tactic is patently effective; the cost to self-realization is, however, not inconsiderable.

These individuals possess a personality structure which continually arranges for their defeat, although consciously they desperately strive to realize themselves, even appearing "selfish" to the casual observer, by virtue of their clinging to every passing straw for support of their faltering ego and career. For example, one sales manager used every available tactic—fair and otherwise—to obtain a minor promotion; and a quite attractive young lady went to great lengths to obtain a marriage proposal. The fruits of this promotion were, however, only ashes in the mouth of this extremely bright young man, since he actually preferred an entirely different kind of work; and although the marriage proposal was indeed a feather in the lady's cap, the man was highly unsuitable as a life companion. Both incidents illustrate tactical success and strategic failure. In the course of a lifetime, the sum of such "successes" is one enormous failure.

Many self-defeatists are so highly gifted that they "get along" in life, or even appear successful. But if their achievements are viewed in the context of their capabilities —then their underachievement becomes apparent. Their interpersonal relations come to serve as a key to their lives. If a man tied a stone around his neck before attempting to swim a swift river, the self-defeat would be obvious. Less obvious, but none the less real, are the "stones" such people tie to themselves when they choose a partner for a business venture, or a mate in marriage. One such person, in planning an important move in his career, remarked that he would choose a certain colleague to look after an important phase of the venture. It developed that this colleague could not be depended upon to do anything at all; that the patient was quite aware of the man's irresponsibility; that the patient could easily have looked after this important phase of the project himself; and that the choice of this colleague, for this important phase, could have been dictated by no weighty consideration—other than insuring the sinking of this particular venture at the time of its launching.

The self-defeatist often makes flagrantly poor decisions regarding the important issues of his life. He will, for example, seriously consider and accept an overseas assignment consuming a number of years of his life. It develops that these years were crucial for essential phases of his self-realization; that reason required their being spent close to home; that this decision cost several years of wasted effort; that he actually had been in possession of all the information required for a wise decision at this point, but that for some unknown reason he chose to do the wrong thing. Such choice is typical: success in the trivia of existence; failure regarding its essentials.

The ingenuity shown in pursuing the non-creative path is striking. One student appeared to be entirely without gifts when it came to writing a term paper and submitting it on time through the usual channels. But his genius for cajoling professors into granting extra time, and for conniving to copy the work of others, would make for an interesting volume in itself.

The self-defeatist tends to expose himself to humiliation and attack, and although well-protected in many of his contacts with the world, suffers from a blind-spot in some particular area of his life, by which he is made continually vulnerable. He may present himself as a "poor soul," or as "pitiable," in situations where past experience has shown such a role to bring a harvest of ridicule and abuse. Or he may persist in being completely "transparent" and artless, in situations requiring tactful obliqueness. It is chronic "bad luck," he believes, which prevents his success. This particular illusion is an early casualty to successful analysis, where his active courting of failure stands out as a consistent personality trend.

These individuals often provoke others into abusing them. They cultivate their own "hangmen"—to use Nietzsche's phrase. They may perceive that a particular way of reacting to people provokes abuse—later heaped upon their heads—yet they persist in this behavior, and needless to say, continue to suffer repetitions of abuse. One man remained for many years at a place of employment where he had been both underpaid and severely abused. When asked why he had remained there so long, his insight extended only to this remark: "I was afraid to move!"

They are often imprudent in the handling of resources. Although aware of how much more pleasant life would be if a minimal amount were saved, they somehow cannot hold on to enough of their earnings, and suffer, again and again, the humiliation of borrowing from friends. They are prone to perfectionism. And their perfectionism may be prone to a failure in achievement. The painter mixes many pigments, and does little more; the writer tears up page after page of manuscript, and "starts over" interminably. A subtly undermining self-doubt saps their potential and energies in the name of perfection. They procrastinate. The student delays submitting a paper until after the time due, and incurs a penalty. The copywriter keeps the agency waiting and loses an account. The salesman simply "cannot" arise until half the morning is gone. They often display a need to oppose others—to have their own way—to an extent which may appear bizarre. A small contractor who had difficulty in paying his bills because of slow business received an order over the phone. Being busy with something at the moment, he said he would phone back "after lunch." "Some lunch!" he later told me. "That was two months ago, and I haven't called him back yet!"

Or take the example of the college student who has been told by his instructor to prepare for an examination by reading a certain chapter of a book. You may guess that this particular student read every chapter of the book *except* the one assigned—and, of course, did poorly on the examination.

Why such self-defeating negativism? The contractor shrugged and said that "Somehow, something always came up—and I just never got around to it." The student smirked as he recalled how every chapter (other than the one assigned) seemed fascinating to him—and he simply could not bring himself to read the assigned portion. Neither one could offer a truly sufficient explanation for this unreasonable oppositionalism; but we shall analyze the problem later, and reach a comprehension of actual operating causes.

Good fortune often poses severe difficulties for self-defeatists. They are frequently thrown into bouts of anxiety and dread when the beneficial and pleasurable fall into their lap. An account executive panicked when an unexpected turn of events brought him a sizeable increase in income, and opportunities for the future; whereas repeated failures in life had never upset him half as much.

Sensuous and sensual pleasures are craved, but can be enjoyed only under conditions which entail concomitant or subsequent suffering. Self-defeatists become tense and

anxious when they attempt to do anything truly constructive. When piddling away their time on trivia, their functioning is relatively smooth and pleasurable; but when they
sit down seriously to accomplish something essential to
their progress, quite severe anxiety is unleashed from deep
within. One gifted writer related: "I sat down to work at
my story—and I became terribly frightened. . . . I had the
image—that if I offered what I had, the multitude would
tear me to pieces for what I had to say. . . . And yet it's all
so stupid. . . . I said to myself: 'What have I to fear? I am
actually in my own place, doing what I am perfectly free
to do.'—And yet I felt like I was doing some horrible
thing."

They often suffer guilt when they plan creative effort.
Unreasonable as it obviously is, the very acts and processes
of successful achievement are associated by them with
doing something "bad" and "evil"—with doing something
for which they are likely to be severely punished. And yet
they are often severely over-competitive. "Wherever I
go—I am always competing and covering up," one self-
defeatist discovered; "I never am just myself!" Another
reported: "I have a tremendous ambition to get ahead. . . .
And I think I want *too much*."

Our culture provides increasing pressure toward conformity and stereotype, as witness the clothes we wear and
the thoughts we express; for there are intrinsic dangers in
being original or "different." But the wine of life requires
the ingredient of freedom to deviate from the herd-path;
and each person generally uses his intelligence so as to
conform only so far as he must. Not so the self-defeatist:
for as he often opposes without rational basis, so does
he frequently bend the knee unnecessarily, when external
realities do not really demand it of him.

There is often extreme submissiveness to the will of

another, a willingness to comply with a partner's demands, however unreasonable. The inroads upon one's privacy, independence, and self-respect which attend such submissiveness often border upon the bizarre.

The instance comes to mind of the husband who, throughout twenty years of marriage, had "permitted" his wife to defeat and humiliate him in every way—the typical yet extreme "henpecked husband." This particular husband did not only "permit" such engulfing of his will, but rather had actively gone about through the years to force his wife into thus abusing him. Of course, the story does not end here, for he—as is usually the case in such instances of self-defeat—was doing many subtle but destructive things to "even the score" with his wife.

Thus, they may manifest a compulsive conformity which stands in strange contrast to a coexisting compulsive oppositionalism. Both the excessive need to comply and the excessive need to oppose operate automatically and rigidly, as if pressured by a mighty inner stream which cannot be deflected or guided by the force of reason. These two opposing compulsive trends alternate in function, adding to the inconsistencies of their lives.

Self-defeatists recoil from the central urge to master life, from the natural curiosity to explore all the abilities and dimensions of selfhood in the world. They withdraw to peripheral and non-essential areas of existence. And their repeated efforts to "achieve" in these restricted areas—even if successful—would still be essentially self-defeat; for the "successful" salesman is still a failure in life if in his heart he has strongly yearned to do creative writing, and if his natural endowments equip him eminently for such writing. They tend to be plagued by feelings of inferiority. No matter how gifted or beautiful they are, they tend to feel inadequate and undesirable, feeling it to be but a matter of time before others come to the same opinion of them. There is a functional loss in flexibility of approach to a problem. Their rigidity stems from dynamics which we shall later comprehend; and this rigidity cripples that openness of outlook which is so essential to the creative approach. There is an impoverishment of personality, a "shut-upness," an "unfreedom," as the insightful Danish philosopher Kierkegaard phrased it. While these people may sometimes display their inability to achieve most clearly in their work history, the underlying forces and related inhibitions are bound also to operate in other areas of their being, and to manifest their influence in other facets of personality.

There is often a reluctance to look squarely at one's life, to examine it closely: "I do not try any more to analyze my life in terms of 'contentment' or 'self-fulfillment'—for if I did, my feelings would be unbearable," is the way one reported it. Yet, there is a gnawing feeling of hollowness—of being a "sham," of being but an actor playing a role, or, as one young man perceived it: "I feel like a stranger—a stranger to others and a stranger to myself." And there is often a critical deficiency in the *positive* quality of one's orientation to life. When the pressures and demands made by life are sufficiently severe, a man's energies may be consumed in simply keeping his head above water, so to speak—in completing essential training or apprenticeship, and in paying accumulating bills. Under such circumstances, he simply does not possess time or inclination to evaluate where he is going, or to think of his years in terms of fulfillment and self-realization.

But when—as sometimes happens near the middle of one's life—the pressures of becoming "established" are relieved, and the individual has the time and energy to reflect upon his life-situation—then there sometimes emerges the terrible realization that he has somehow lost his way, that he has been traveling a senseless road for many years —that his present life-situation is hollow and meaningless, and that further "successes" in the same way of life will only mean eventual long term, over-all defeat. In response to the acute pressures and exigencies of life, the man has run hard along certain pathways, apparently being "successful" in achieving symbols of status and "security"; but when the pressures of anxiety are thus relieved, and he can look more objectively upon his life-situation, its essential emptiness casts a shadow of futility upon the road ahead. As one "successful" administrator at this stage of his life reported sadly, "No—I haven't any 'star.' But I *did* have one—once!"

Just where the "star" was lost is difficult to determine. "When I was a boy," recalled a scientist who characteristically remained at positions far below his level of capability, "I used to love to plan where I was going. I used to get a real thrill out of planning my development—and then trying to do something about it. But somehow I lost the urge. . . ." For he had indeed come gradually to stumble blindly through life, permitting his career to be molded by external pressures and inner self-defeating trends.

When is self-realization stifled? And when is it simply a defect falling within "normal limits," so to speak? The answer seems to lie in the differential between potentialities and accomplishments, in the gap between capacities for creative life and the levels of actually realized capabilities.

Mature creative selfhood is obviously not identical with culturally defined levels of adulthood; for who can doubt that the vast majority of adults in our time have realized but a small fraction of their positive potentialities, and are but inferior caricatures of their creative possibilities? Our yardstick for detecting stifled selfhood must therefore reside within the individual, in the potentials we sense to exist within him, and in the operation of identified hampering influences upon his optimal fruition.

So now, having described patterns of reaction which accompany dwarfed self-realization and self-defeat, we turn to explore and identify their underlying causes. We shall seek a clear and relatively integrated understanding of this crucially important problem—important to the individual as well as to society—the problem of self-defeat versus successful self-realization in life.

NOTES

[1] The reader interested in a carefully documented analysis of self-and-other defeat in the areas of psychotherapy, philosophy, and mythology, will find it in my book *The Urge to Mass Destruction* (New York: Grune and Stratton, 1957).

[2] A summary of these writings may be found in my paper "The Problem of the Defeating Patient in Psychotherapy" in *American Journal of Psychotherapy*, Vol. 8 (1954), pp. 703–718.

[3] This area is explored in my paper "The Concept of Satan as An Aid to the Understanding of Human Destructiveness" in *Journal of Religious Thought*, Vol. 13 (1956), pp. 93–109.

[4] I shall frequently refer to illustrative case material selected from my own and my colleagues' clinical experience in counseling and psychotherapy over the past twenty years. While these case illustrations are true in all essential respects, I have altered non-essential characteristics so as to render patient identification impossible.

II

HOSTILITY IN DARKNESS

"Anger rusts the intellect," runs a medieval Jewish proverb. And the pity of it is this: Anger properly employed actually assists self-realization—is grist for the mill of creative endeavor; whereas anger improperly employed undermines the inner freedom to make the most of oneself in life.

Our experiences in psychotherapy prove repeatedly that people whose self-realization has been impoverished over many years generally possess an enormous quantity of submerged hostility. As therapy progresses, this subterranean hostility emerges; and in due course—after the emergence and integration of this unspeakably intense resentment—there is a rebirth of creative hope and personal fulfillment.

It was to this dynamic of "repressed hatred" that the psychoanalyst Wilhelm Reich pointed, in his explanation of the "negative therapeutic reaction." It was at the door of intense but unconscious resentment that he and other noted psychoanalysts placed much of the blame for the curtailment of the personal freedom to succeed encountered in the psychotherapeutic situation. One patient, emerging from such a condition, reported: "My hatred is surging out like a tremendous eruption of mud and rock. It is like something that has been smoldering for years—and now is bursting forth."

If this repressed hatred, this unconscious hostility, holds such signal importance for one's self-realization, we would be wise to know its ways well. Let us, therefore, explore the roots and ramifications of this unconscious resentment.

THE MEANING OF "UNCONSCIOUS HOSTILITY"

First, let us develop a few general ideas about the meaning of the term "unconscious." For much of the practical meaningfulness of what follows in this book will depend upon a grasp of the significance of this concept.

We might start by defining what is meant by *conscious,* and here Sigmund Freud was definitive: "Now let us call 'conscious' the conception which is present to our consciousness and of which we are aware, and let this be the only meaning of the term 'conscious.' "

Consciousness—that of which we are aware—is but an infinitesimal part of our mind. The vast reservoir of tendencies and learnings, the huge hinterland of potentials for response, belongs to the unconscious. For as Sigmund Freud defined: "Everything else that is mental," everything residing outside of consciousness, "is in our view *unconscious.*"

One qualification is necessary: Freud differentiated elements which can readily be brought into consciousness, as by one's own association of ideas, and he called these "preconscious." He distinguished these preconscious elements from those ideas and feelings which cannot ordinarily be brought into awareness by one's own association of ideas—and these latter elements alone are now termed the "unconscious." And when we use the term "unconscious" from now on, we shall generally do so in its latter and more restricted sense. It implies that there are inner forces which push this unconscious material back, and which prevent its rise to consciousness, in spite of its intensity and activity—giving it that "certain dynamic character" Freud described.

"But," one might counter, "if something does not come into your awareness—how do you know that it exists at all? How do you know that the unconscious is real, and not a figment of some fevered imagination?"

The answer—appreciated some time before our modern experimental validation of the unconscious came into being—was put into words eloquently by Freud, although the case had earlier been made more crudely: "We call 'unconscious' any mental process the existence of which we are obliged to assume—because, for instance, we infer it in some way from its effects—but of which we are not directly aware."

For example, if an individual continually falls into pits he could easily have avoided, and if he is not aware of any related motive, we infer the existence of an unconscious wish to suffer misfortune. Or, if he continually suffers nightmares and palpitations, but is not aware, in his usual waking state, of any fears or insecurities—we infer the existence of unconscious anxiety. Moreover, repeated clinical observation of the emergence of inner elements during the course of psychotherapy tends to corroborate the validity of such inferences.

In addition, ingenious modern experiments have supported Freud in this conception of the unconscious. One such research, by the psychologists[1] Robert A. McCleary and Richard S. Lazarus, demonstrated that we can react strongly to an emotion-inducing stimulus—even when we are not aware of the nature of that stimulus.

They demonstrated this important understanding in the following way: Two sets of nonsense syllables were selected—syllables such as "YILIM," "ZIFIL," "GEXAX" —syllables not likely to possess any pre-existing emotional meaning for subjects. Then, the subjects were conditioned to expect an electric shock when one series of syllables was shown, but not so with the other series of syllables; and this was accomplished simply by the repeated application of mild electric shock whenever a syllable of the "shock" series was exposed to view.

Now, when we react emotionally, there is generally some change in the degree to which we perspire through the skin. Since skin which perspires more conducts electricity more readily than that which perspires less, by applying a regulated amount of fairly weak electric current between two electrodes attached to some portion of the skin (such as that of the hand), and by using sensitive instruments for detecting changes in the actual flow of electricity, the investigators could avail themselves of an excellent indicator of changes in emotional status—termed the "psychogalvanic reflex" or the "galvanic skin reflex."

Then a tachistoscope was used to regulate the time during which the nonsense syllables were exposed to the subject's view. The tachistoscope is simply a device for regulating the amount of time a shutter is open, and in this way permits an accurate regulating of exposure time—in this instance, the time during which the nonsense syllables were exposed.

And now, here is the point, and an important point it is: Even when the exposure time was so short that the subject could not possibly have identified accurately what he was momentarily looking at, he tended to respond *emotionally* when exposed to the shock-conditioned words, as indicated by his galvanic skin response. That is, while he was not *aware* that he was viewing shock-conditioned syllables, his inner reaction—manifested in his perspiration rate—indicated clearly that he appreciated the shock-associated meaning of what he was viewing, and reacted accordingly —without conscious identification of the shock-stimulus. On the other hand, when the exposed syllables were not shock-associated, no such autonomic reaction tended to be induced.

Notice how analogous this is to the situation of the human mind. Each of us has a built-in functioning tachistoscope, so to speak. Freud termed such a function "censorship." But regardless of its name, there is undoubtedly something inside which regulates the degree to which we can perceive inner truth—ideas and feelings we truly possess, ideas and feelings whose inner existence can be demonstrated in a number of ways, such as by hypnosis or narcosis—but of which we are not aware in our ordinary waking state.

Hence our conclusion: If we react emotionally to these inner elements, *without being aware of just what these elements are,* as McCleary and Lazarus demonstrated to be the case with an external tachistoscope, then our lives and behavior may well be largely determined by unconscious elements and processes, even though we are not aware of the natures of those elements and processes. Remarkable indeed is the way such experimental findings have validated Freud's bold formulations!

Now, we speak of *the* unconscious, as if it were a location or space in the mind—the "unconscious mind." Actually, the unconscious refers to *process* rather than to a thing in itself. But we shall continue to refer to *the* unconscious, since it facilitates communication.

We speak also of the "unconscious," as against the "conscious," as if either were an all-or-none thing. Actually there is no sharp demarcation between the two. A continuum exists: Some elements of mind are readily viewed in consciousness; others are viewed only with extreme difficulty, and under special conditions; some are never seen at all.

The much employed concept of "repression," which was for Freud the "foundation stone" of his understanding of the neuroses, is pertinent here. Again, we have a process, and as Freud defines it, the "essence" of repression lies simply in the function of rejecting and "keeping something out of consciousness." Such repression differs from ordinary "forgetting." Forgetting occurs with lack of use over a period of time, that is, due to the absence of reinforcement by recent experiences; whereas a repressed response is actively blocked from emerging, and may break into awareness when appropriate conditions exist, without any relearning. Repression also differs from "suppression." For the latter denotes a consciously directed inhibiting of elements, a conscious pushing down of material; whereas repression operates without reference to any conscious effort or awareness. Repression is not a thing done only once, and thereby completed. It is rather something which requires continuous expenditure of effort. Thus, repression is costly to the individual, being a steady drain on his energy for the function of "putting down."

"If it is so costly to the organism, why does it take place at all?" you may ask. The answer is fairly clearcut: Repression is a *functioning defense*. Each of us must discipline his impulses, else we could not get along within a social group. If an impulse, such as a sexual or hostile one, is known from experience and past punishments to be "dangerous" and anxiety-provoking, one can inhibit awareness of the impulse, and thus lessen the chances of acting it out—and of incurring the danger and the eventual punishment. In brief, repression serves to keep the rejected impulses from motility. It blocks the tendency to discharge.

Now, hostility is precisely the sort of impulse likely to be associated with the anxiety of "danger," with the anticipation of severe punishment, and therefore is likely to be repressed. The child loves the parent in some measure, and believes that he is dependent upon the parent for life itself. And who can be intensely angry with the loved one—the very one whose love and protection are sensed to be needed for survival—without experiencing severe anxiety along with the hostility? In addition, our culture reinforces the extreme "danger" associated in the child's mind with hostility. For in modern Western culture, and especially in middle-class segments of it, two varieties of impulses least tolerated are visible hostility and sex. It is for the open expression of these that the child meets the most severe punishment and withdrawal of affection. As a result, the child learns, quite early in life, to repress hostility toward those close to him, even though they are the very ones who arouse his resentment.

As to the role of developmental frustration in the causation of hostility, Sigmund Freud repeatedly illustrated this causal interrelationship in his case material. The American psychologist, John Dollard, consequently formulated his frustration-aggression principle: *The existence of frustration always leads to some form of aggression.* This holds for all needs. The more central and essential the need whose gratification is thwarted, the more intense the resulting hostility and aggression are likely to be.

A small amount of frustration adds zest to life, and may

actually spur growth and successful creativity. But severe or prolonged frustration may cause rigidity in one's approach to life, and may therefore materially curtail the developing child's opportunity for effective personality development. It unleashes considerable hostility, much of which may remain unconscious. The child who is frustrated regarding essential needs, for example, may evidence bedwetting long after his sphincter control has actually been well established, and may manifest intense hostility in a number of other ways, while being aware of relatively little of this feeling.

Of the many needs which may be frustrated, and whose frustration may unleash intense hostility, the need for love and acceptance is in our time and culture most often in the key causal position. This is so, largely because our culture fosters intense competition and egotism, so that parents tend to possess what that astute critic of our culture, Karen Horney, has termed—and employed as the title of her classic—"The Neurotic Personality of Our Time."

The chief feature of this neurotic personality lies in the inability to love; consequently, the developing child is frustrated in its need to relate in love. Horney said it this way: "The main reason why a child does not receive enough warmth and affection lies in the parents' incapacity to give it on account of their own neuroses." This is what Dr. Horney termed "the basic evil" in our time—the "lack of genuine warmth and affection."

By way of illustration, one man recalled: "My father was the kind of man who made my mother get out of bed to brew his tea—when she was ill. . . . He was partly responsible for her death." Such early cruelty leaves a deep scar. This man literally seethed with hatred toward figures of authority from that period on, yet was not aware of his hatred toward these extra-familial figures, nor of the many self-crippling tactics to which it compelled him.

We all possess ambivalence toward others. That is, on a deep level, we tend to hate as well as to love every living thing we know. Growing up and maturing involves a reconciliation of this conflict between love and hate. Accordingly, the adequately mature parent should possess reasonable freedom from ambivalence toward the child. That is, he should have made his peace with his resentments, so as to be sufficiently free to love those who need and depend upon his love. But our competitive age does not lend itself to such adequate resolution of this ambivalence. It rather tends to fill the man with unresolved resentments.

The result is often this: The parent remains markedly ambivalent toward all—including his own child; the child is therefore bitterly frustrated with respect to valid needs for love and acceptance; accordingly, hate springs from this frustration of his love needs. Such frustration, moreover, does not extinguish either the need for love or the hatred consequent to its denial. Rather, clinical evidence indicates that the denied need for love persists in infantile and childish form far longer and with more intensity than where adequate satisfaction is encountered. And this persisting need, in a milieu of persisting frustration, results in persisting hostility. The repression of this need for love and consequent hostility, the driving down into the unconscious of both the wish to be loved and the hatred because of its thwarting, makes neither of these less real, but only more viciously effective in undermining the inner freedom to function creatively.

The situation comes to mind of two gifted sisters who grew up in the same household, reared by parents who were essentially overwhelmed by life, and who were no longer able to love. Both sisters grew on a regimen of parental duty, mixed with conflicting parental resentment and guilt. This constellation is not unusual in our society; but what is unusual is the extreme disparity between the subsequent careers of the two children: One, who openly faced the household situation, together with her extreme resulting hostility, developed into a highly accomplished artist. Her sister, however, who could not tolerate awareness of hostility—but who was clearly as intelligent, and probably as gifted—developed little more than an elaborate system of obsessive-compulsive defenses. The energies which were channeled into creativity in one instance found expression in neurosis in the other. And the governing factor making for this distinction appears clearly to have been the ability to face hostility; for when the second, through psychotherapy, became more tolerant of her resentment, her obsessive-compulsive symptomatology dropped off markedly, and her creativity blossomed.

The child is surprisingly effective in recognizing love. His vocabulary is limited, as are his ideational understandings. But he senses clearly, in his feelings, whether or not he is truly accepted; and is not deceived, in the long run, by pretended exhibitions. His pattern of relating to the parents will indicate clearly what he senses their own feelings to be.

Sometimes sibling rivalry enters as a cause of hostility. But when one child feels he must compete with another for the affection of a parent, the quality of the parent's affection should be scrutinized, since the parent who loves with reasonable freedom from ambivalence generally has sufficient feeling to go around. When children compete for it, one might suspect its essential absence. We do not tend to compete for that which is abundant.

Parental overprotection sometimes poses a paradox,

since it often coexists with a petulant hostility in the child, and therefore raises the question as to why such obvious and overly ample care and attention should beget hostility. But the paradox dissolves when one realizes that over solicitousness in a parent is generally a façade which hides actual rejection and hatred. The loving are not ostentatiously unselfish. The overprotective parent is likely to be the subtly, overly *dominant* parent; and the dominance is apt to be linked to intense repressed hostility toward the object of over care and over concern.

There is a need for a "larger existence." There is a deep hunger for living *with* others—for not being alone. This is not—as we tend to believe in our extroverted age—a thing of physical proximity; it is rather a sensed relatedness in mutual constructiveness, an inner understanding: "If I will observe ordinary standards of decency toward you —then you will be similarly constructive toward me."

One truly tough veteran of Guadalcanal, in the course of his psychotherapy for persistent anxiety attacks, remarked: "The reason I explode is that I try to be nice to people—and they're mean to me!" Less eloquent than Job, his was essentially the same grief and the same resentment. Indifferent or arbitrary discipline in the home has been shown to be the most outstanding apparent cause of juvenile delinquency; and childhood disciplinary problems in school have been linked to undemocratic discipline in the home. What is the element possessed in common by these diverse illustrations? To me it is this: There is a deep and intense need within each of us for a larger existence characterized by ordinary decency and justice; when this need is frustrated, we all react with bitter resentment.

There is an urge to realize oneself, to fulfill the promise sensed in youth. And to the degree that each of us feels thwarted, deflected, and twisted from the optimal fruition of our potentials, to that extent does each possess a reservoir of resentment from whose subterranean depths flow the energies to defeat our own efforts in life.

So much for the generators of unconscious hostility. Let us now see what the patterns are whereby such hostility is discharged; patterns which curtail one's ability to succeed in the realization of life's creative possibilities.

SELF-DEFEATING OUTLETS

We all need some form of discharge for our resentments. Yet we somehow tend to fall into the error of believing that strong resentment may be swallowed whole, for as long a period of time as one chooses, without disturbing other areas of personality. Actually, the evidence indicates that the resentment and its associated energies *are* dissipated in some way—even if it be so covert a way as the mediating outpouring of adrenalin into the blood stream, or the violent contraction of arterial wall musculature.

The more overt and obvious ways of dissipating hostility's energies are more dramatic. One woman reported: "I became so angry with my mother—that I actually slapped *myself!*" Another, whose long-repressed hatred gradually emerged during psychotherapy, began to bite her lips continually whenever engrossed in thought—that is, she turned her hostility back upon the "hostile mouth" that was increasingly prone to speak long-forbidden thoughts. And suicides provide frequent illustration of the self-destructive extremes to which people will go in order to vent their resentments: They destroy themselves in order to strike out at someone else.

But we are concerned with less clear-cut, less final forms

of self-destruction than suicide. And in this section we shall now consider a number of non-creative and self-defeating patterns of discharge for one's hostility—and primarily, for one's *unconscious* hostility.

These non-creative patterns take many forms. One may, for example, inhibit awareness of feeling. Then, the inhibited hostility is left to find other channels for its gradual dissipation. Inhibition sufficiently strong to prevent awareness, and operating automatically, constitutes the *repression* we discussed earlier.

Various physiological functions may absorb this inner resentment, such as a continuous misuse of various muscles in spasms, or functional circulatory alterations—changes in rate of heartbeat, and so on. In such reactions, the mental content of the anger is warded off from consciousness, while the physical concomitants of the emotion take place to varying extents.

When hostility rises above the individual's level of tolerance, there is danger to self-realization, for undesirable methods of relieving this pent-up hostility may be invoked —methods which seriously undercut the unfolding of latent powers. For example, the inhibited resentment may turn against oneself, and depression may result, with its general apathy, impaired self-concept, fatigue, and discouragement. Or, in turning against oneself, one's work habits and career may be the target of the aggressiveness, resulting in "occupational inhibition," such as "writer's block."

When such resentment builds up, although we are hardly aware of its existence, there often occurs an undermining of one's will to engage in long-term creative work. For mounting hostility, even though largely unconscious, craves a quick release; but work and protracted effort do not promise such rapidity, and therefore tend to fall victim to feelings of lassitude and "fatigue." Through such *non-*

functioning, there is at least a sort of rebellion against the frustrating world, and therefore some sort of temporary relief for one's hostility (but unfortunately, a form of relief which seriously detracts from the realization of creative potentials).

To such inwardly hostile people, working effectively tends to unleash a marked depression; whereas, when they are idle, the depression is relieved. The determination of this phenomenon is unquestionably multiple, but one essential factor appears to be this: When they sit idly—at the very times when some authority figure expects them to work—this represents in itself a directing of hostility *outward;* hence the temporary lifting of feelings of depression. For depression represents essentially a turning of hostility inward toward the self, and it therefore follows that any measure which deflects hostility outward tends temporarily to relieve the depression.

But the pressure to "act out" resentment is natural, and strong. For example, when we are intensely angry, we tend toward outbursts of temper. But it is dangerous to act out resentment, whether it be in temper outbursts or in violent action. The infant and child, especially in the sort of hostile and frustrating home we have described, find it impossible to adequately communicate their resentment in direct form, for the direct expression of hostility against the parent or authority figure is surely fraught with danger. The egotistical and power-oriented adult is hardly likely to let such expression of hostility go by without severe retribution. One man reported of his childhood, "When my father was home I couldn't even *indicate* my anger. . . . If I showed the slightest sign of anger, he would beat me."

But the frustrations we have described are intense. The child *is* angry. What is he to do with his anger?

A "solution" to this dilemma is unfortunately discovered early in life by many of us; and this solution is predicated upon the following irrefutable premise: "My parents want me to *function*."

Mother, and father too, unquestionably want the child to cooperate in performing basic functions of life: to eat, and to eat enough; to control his elimination; to learn to talk; and later, to learn the three R's at school and get the grades that will cause them to feel proud.

So now, how to fight the parents? How to vent resentment against them? Simply by this stratagem: *Do not function!*

If the child does not eat, mother is perplexed; if he does not keep his food down, the whole household is thrown into an uproar; and if he does not learn his three R's quickly, father is visibly uneasy. This, therefore, is a basic element in all our repertoires: "I vent my hostility toward parental figures through *my* not functioning, through *my* not living properly." Moreover, this is a relatively "safe" way to vent hostility toward the parents, for it carries its own built-in camouflage: The child is hurting himself, too. That is, if the child "cannot" eat properly, he thwarts the parent; but his own loss is so obvious as to throw the true significance of the act out of meaningful focus. Similarly, if he suffers from bed-wetting, his own discomfort and humiliation are so clear as to hide the hostility so often inherent in the act. By "bleeding a little," so to speak, he causes his attack upon the parent to appear accidental, or beyond his control. Defeat of the "other" is accomplished fairly safely through self-and-other defeat.

All of us learn in childhood that we can "get back" at others by defeating ourselves. It is an element of childhood's repertoire of mechanisms for dealing with life. And thus the stage is set for the utilization of self-defeat as a way of venting unconscious resentment in life. For, in time, these self-defeating patterns sink from consciousness, and are used with little or no awareness of their essential meanings. Yet they remain as part of our repertoire for meeting life, to be called forth when the occasion demands.

Actually, self-defeat is always self-and-other defeat. For there is always someone who depends upon the self-defeatist, or whose feelings would be hurt in learning of a suicide or self-injury. Even, in the instance of the friendless man, self-destruction removes the possibility of service to other friendless living things. Therefore, while we shall often employ the term "self-defeat" to facilitate communication, yet we shall know that this is always properly self-and-other defeat.

Normally, we all want to move ahead, to realize the "highest" in ourselves. This is surely a powerful human need. But a threat to one's self-realization exists in the following: In our repertoire of responses for dealing with life, we all have a hierarchy with respect to "goodness" for self-realization.

When angered by a neighbor's inconsiderate action, for example, there are many ways in which one could respond to the situation. At one extreme, one could assault him—using brute force. Higher on the scale, one could bide one's time and get "revenge"—in a way less likely to break the law and incur damage to oneself. Higher still, one might seek to understand his behavior, and thus to find peaceful and perhaps even friendly coexistence. The point is that when we are angry each of us is capable of a wide variety of responses. And these responses represent a hierarchy with respect to goodness for self-realization.

Some are severely hurtful to the self, whereas others are actually helpful, assisting us to realize the best within ourselves.

The highest form of expression our resentments can take is surely creativity. The man who can use his hurts and dissatisfactions as motives for changing life in some helpful and useful way is indeed fortunate. The creative approach unquestionably helps self-realization most. At the other extreme, down at the bottom of this hierarchy of responses—in terms of maturation and self-realization—is some form of self-defeat.

We have already seen how self-defeat came to be a meaningful way in which the child vented resentment toward his parent. We have followed the "logic" of how this "perversion" of life's energies becomes part of a child's hierarchy of responses for meeting his world; and we know that a living thing does *not* want to defeat itself; rather, it wants to realize the best and highest in itself. But this urge to realize oneself clashes with the immediate pressure to give vent to underlying resentment.

So we have a real and consequential inner conflict. And the thing that often tips the balance away from self-realization and toward self-defeat is this: Unconscious resentment builds up in the individual to a point at which he can no longer contain himself, and in one form or another the underlying resentment, to some degree, breaks through as self-defeat.

Of course, we do not generally employ this mode of venting hostility, because of the obvious hurt to oneself it necessarily entails. But here is the point: If unconscious hostility builds up sufficiently, and over a long period of time, we all are susceptible to this sort of regression to the infantile formulation—to the venting of hostility *through harming one's own opportunities for self-fulfill-*

ment. It is the last avenue left open to the despairing personality; it can—and often does—undermine the very will to live. It is the ultimate way to "even the score" with the many who have been unloving, who "drove me to this." In brief, it follows the formula: "I vent my hostility through not being able to deal with life; through not being able to function as a human being in society."

The most extreme form taken by this pattern is suicide. It is the ultimate "revenge" against the insufficiently loving parent, or against whoever touched off the final frenzied rage.

A less extreme form taken by the emerging resentment is severe breakdown, emotional illness of sufficient severity to require hospitalization. We are reared, women especially, to feel no hostility, but rather to be continually "understanding" and "pleasant"; and the particularly pathetic part of this psychological picture is that some people require a "nervous breakdown" before they can experience or express their resentment at all fully.

One lovely person, a truly fine and considerate lady, could not countenance her intense resentment against an unusually brutish family group—that is, when she possessed her ordinary personality. But every once in a while, she would shed her inhibitions in a personality breakdown, would rave in a fury, and finally require hospitalization. It was only through undergoing the extreme pain and humiliation of a psychotic reaction that she could permit herself to give vent to her resentment and to point an accusing finger against the monstrous household from which she took asylum.

One principle which emerges is this: If hostility is pent up in sufficient intensity and over a sufficiently long period of time, the individual will tend to regress, to go back to a lower level of development, in order to give expression to this pent-up rage. This has been demonstrated experimentally with children, in terms of the level of personality maturity and differentiation shown in play behavior in the face of experimentally regulated irksome frustration. It is also unquestionably true in the areas of personality organization and the level of functioning regarding creative achievement. If one cannot deal adequately with underlying hostility on the basis of adult creativity, one tends to regress, even to the following level of childish meaning: "I make *them* sorry for what they have done by my not functioning properly, by my not living properly, by my breakdown."

Self-defeatists oppose progress in their own therapy. As one man reported, "I have come to label my illness as 'the desire to get even.'" Such people therefore resist getting well, since "not functioning properly" serves to express resentment toward mother and her substitutes. Originally, it was the parent who was to be hurt through the individual's not functioning; and analogous self-defeat has been noted in the clinical situation, where the intensely hostile patient will resist progress in therapy because he senses that in "getting well" he will please the doctor.

As such self-defeatists develop insight into what is really going on in their lives, they make sense out of what had previously seemed senseless childhood behavior. "As a child," such a woman recalled, "I could take a toy that meant a lot to me—and break it! . . . And later, at school, I could take a term paper—a perfectly good paper—and rip it up!" It was such a "ripping up" of her marriage that propelled her toward treatment. The areas she destroyed changed as she grew older; but her approach to life remained essentially the same—self-and-other defeat.

Unconscious resentment may take antisocial form. The so-called kleptomaniac steals the symbols of love and personal goodness which he craves, and has been denied. And if the thief is caught and punished, he has succeeded in casting society and its penal institutions into the role of the unloving parent, whom he can now hate the more readily for being so unsympathetic and cruel. Not that society does not warrant some degree of indictment in its own right; but the phenomena of recidivism and hatred of policemen appear consistent with our clinically derived understanding of the need to become involved with an "unloving parent"—to have a target for relieving the pressure of largely unconscious hatred.

The venting of hostility is by no means limited to active procedures. In the phenomena of severe mental illness, for example, hostility may be vented by the catatonic schizophrenic patient in either a frenzy of hyperactivity, or—and this is the point—through *failure* to do what is expected of him, as in the catatonic stupor. The extreme conditions of mental illness are helpful in exposing to view those forces which are also at work in the sane. Specifically, the phases of catatonia, which frequently alternate in the same individual, underline the principle that one can express hostility and oppositionalism through either extremely *high* activity or extremely *low* activity; through either being openly aggressive, or through appearing to be extremely passive.

Similarly—in less obviously sick behavior—the venting of hostility may be carried out by "passive" means. That is, one can express resentment through *failing* to do what is expected of one. And these passive techniques for venting hostility can be sorely self-defeating.

Procrastination is one such device of passivity. The salesman who "cannot" arise until half the morning is gone, the student who always manages to turn in required papers several days past the deadline, are examples. This quite effective method for frustrating others carries, however, an obvious penalty to one's own level of functioning. We have also previously noted "perfectionism" as another method. It is often thinly veiled oppositionalism (combined, of course, with anxiety and other forces). One quite gifted musician whose reputation with producers had suffered materially through the employment of this device came to understand: "I realize that my perfectionism is really in the service of my hostility. . . . that when I piddle with something in order to 'perfect' it—what I am really doing is holding people up."

Subtle non-cooperation may cause many a gifted child to appear feeble-minded, since it often finds expression in oppositionalism toward learning (toward pleasing the parents who want to show the child off). Analogously, in large bureaucratic organizations, demoralized personnel often use a subtle "slow-down" to even the score with management. The self-defeat in both instances is obvious.

The urge to vengeance nurtures self-defeating patterns. Children who actively rebel against learning and healthful maturation, so as to avenge themselves upon an insufficiently loving parent, are often seen at the clinic. Adults, too, will refrain from taking a much needed step toward creativity because that step would benefit the parent or some parent surrogate. One such young man simply would not take notes in class, knowing that his parents would be "punished" by college grades that fell far below his potentials. From the cradle to the grave, the "inability to function" serves as an outlet for hostility.

An interesting illustration of self-defeat is that of the lovely bride to be, one week before her wedding, whose mother said, "Papa told me that you look drawn. . . . Be sure to get plenty of rest—be sure to look good on Sunday" (her wedding day). And the young lady's reaction? "I

have a feeling I would like to look *grotesque* on Sunday
—I'm so furious!"

You may wonder why this young woman is used as an
illustration in this chapter—which is on hostility that is
largely *unconscious*, whereas this woman was aware of her
strong resentment. The answer is that she (as most of the
people we describe) was in treatment, and that during the
course of such therapy she became aware of feelings that
had formerly operated to produce self-defeat *without* her
awareness.

Such self-defeatists disappoint people in ways which
injure themselves. One young man who harbored intense
hatred against his mother—and therefore against all mother
substitutes, i.e., all women—told of his long difficulty in
finding suitable employment. "My wife gives me the devil,"
he said softly. "She's upset about it." And I need hardly
tell you by now that there was a glint of vindictive pleasure in his eye, "pleasure" of which he was largely unaware.

In order to "spite" such authority figures, a person may
oppose his own opportunities for self-help and advancement. Such self-hurt may be small and token, as in the
instance of the chemist who reported, "I was pleased to
be elected to the chemistry honor society, but I am pleased
not to have bought the key—so that nobody knows about
it"; or as in the instance of the woman who related that
her examining dentist had reported that she possessed "fine
teeth." "And you know," she added, "that was three days
ago, and I haven't brushed my teeth since!" But such occurrences may be considerably more serious, and even
encompass one's whole way of life. In one case, a technician delayed adequately learning job skills for many
years, and this substantially delayed her advancement;
meanwhile, she complained bitterly about the cruel figures

of authority—her supervisors—who retarded her progress. It was only later, after considerable psychotherapy, that she perceived her own motives, and really applied herself to learning her specialty. In another case, a man perpetuated an immature approach to life, for this unquestionably thwarted a mother who had pushed him since childhood toward "successful" competition. It is noteworthy that at those times when authority is particularly provoking and frustrating, the self-damage to personal efficiency is perceptibly increased.

This inner hatred of authority figures hamstrings the freedom to achieve, for successful achievement generally causes some superior to be pleased, be he parent, teacher, employer, or critic. Accordingly, an artist who was accepted as brilliant by competent critics found that she held back her real talent because she simply did not want to *give*. "I use a good part of my energies," she came eventually to see, "in just playing slick tricks. . . . I hate these people so—that I don't *want* to give them anything that's really good."

Such passive-aggressive modes of venting unconscious hostility may be integrated within what we term the "character"—the pattern of acting-out behavior characteristic of the individual. In the official nomenclature of the American Psychiatric Association, such "passive obstructionism"—the expression of aggressiveness through passive measures—characterizes what is termed the "passive-aggressive personality."

Such passive-aggressive personalities show their colors early in treatment. While they may be very charming and pleasant to be with, yet the therapist soon finds that he is working essentially "alone," for they act out this pattern: "I will vent my rage by lying down—by permitting life to run over me." They are essentially "truants" from life. They are the children who won't button their coats on a cold day on the way home from school, feeling, "Mama will be upset when she sees how little I care about my welfare."

One such woman was married and divorced three times; each man was clearly unsuitable for her. It is difficult to pin down the ways in which she closed her eyes when being courted and selecting a mate, but a clear fact is that she refused to have anything to do with the practical arrangements of each marriage, a relative being chosen to deal with the caterer, the florist, and the others involved. In this, she could turn aside from looking after her own interests for fairly "proper" and "respectable" reasons. In therapy, she tried to do the same; to have me do the work for her. Always charming and attractive, the sessions passed quickly and pleasantly. But she never quite comprehended what I said to her. And I, for my part, found myself asking of myself: "What is she *saying?* What is she *really* saying?"

In truth, she was not saying anything—that is, not anything that pertained to her true feelings. She was mentally absent from therapy, as from everything else that really mattered. She brought herself physically to sessions, but removed herself in the more vital sense.

She had been infuriated, as a child, and had learned to deal with it this way: "If mama and papa won't be good to me, and show me a full measure of affection—then I will get even with them, I will get even with life itself—by not looking out for myself. And *they'll* be sorry!" She had good reason to be furious. One can only shake one's head in disbelief at the utter insensitivity of her parents and the cruelty she suffered at their hands. As treatment progressed, she referred from time to time to music lessons that she had desperately yearned for and never gotten.

We should note that her father was quite well-off financially, and the absence of such lessons (which were commonplace in the upper middle-class milieu of her childhood) was the focal point of her inner feelings of being unloved, of not being considered worthy of such expense.

And so she thrust the actual work and responsibility of therapy upon me, or at least tried to. She was going to default—to go through the motions of analyzing her behavior—without really committing herself to the task.

She was, for example, about to change her job, since her employer was going out of business. What did *I* think she should do, she asked. When I returned with "What would *you* really like to do?" she said some unrevealing and equivocal things, and then returned to her original question: What did *I* think she should do? Obviously, she wanted to be out of it. I was to make decisions for her exactly as had those who took care of the arrangements for her marriages. The world was full of "caterers" for her, and of relatives who would deal with the caterers. She would go through marriages, as through therapy, without really getting involved—except in passive-aggression. The marriages had fallen apart and various people were duly "sorry"; therapy was being eased along the same road, to the same sort of ending.

I pressed her to consider what *she* thought best to do. Finally, she admitted that the sensible thing to do was to get another job, similar to the one now ending. Did she enjoy the work? "No, not really," she said. Actually, she despised it. It was drudgery. It did not employ her very considerable intelligence and sensibilities. She came in time to see that she hired herself out as an "office machine," a phrase she used repeatedly thereafter in describing her role in life. But she doggedly resisted appreciating these meanings, and their underlying strategy: "I will permit my life to be curtailed and eventually destroyed; and then the world (my parents) will regret it—and I will thus have my revenge!"

But in time, she analyzed the furies basic to her resistance, and with knowledge came an increased capacity for adjusting her inner emotional needs to the outer conditions of life. She did not cease resenting her early emotional hardship, but found outlets less damaging to the realization of her potentials.

So much for the self-destructive forms taken by hostilities whose causes or effects are not sufficiently appreciated in awareness, by hostilities which are essentially in darkness. We turn now to the investigation of other varieties of forces which curtail the inner freedom to realize the positive potentials of selfhood. And we may be wise to contemplate a verity posed by Pythagoras: "None can be free who is slave to, and governed by, his passions."

NOTES

[1] Robert A. McCleary and Richard S. Lazarus, "Autonomic Discrimination Without Awareness" in *Journal of Personality*, Vol. 18 (1949), pp. 171–179; also an extended report under same title in *Psychological Review*, Vol. 58 (1951), pp. 113–122.

III

INROADS OF ANXIETY

The solution to the "riddle" of anxiety, wrote Freud, "must cast a flood of light upon our whole mental life." Nowhere is this prophecy more meaningful than in the context of self-realization versus self-defeat, for anxiety is a fundamental process of life. It is a common denominator holding the key to the comprehension of all manner of men and behavior, since we all deeply crave inner peace, seek respite from anxiety, and desire "emotional security."

Yet—in defiance of common sense and sanity—the quest for emotional security leads some of us time and again to the brink of personal disaster, and sometimes plunges us irrevocably downward; the yearning for freedom from anxiety may drive us toward making more and more real difficulties for ourselves; the craving for inner peace may propel us forward to the front lines of self-perpetuating, interpersonal "wars."

Therefore, let us explore the roots and ramifications of this irrationality, in order to comprehend how the human urge for emotional security can lead some of us to a continual undermining of the grounds of our real security and to chronic self-defeat.

THE NATURE AND MEANING OF ANXIETY

What do we mean by anxiety? While anxieties may vary greatly in intensity, from a mere qualm to an all-consuming apprehension, they all possess this element in common: *a sense of impending danger.* One feels that something threatening is about to occur. Anxiety is, in Freud's words, "a signal indicating the presence of a danger-situation."

There is an element of helplessness in anxiety. There is the inner impression that the sensed danger is inescapable, that there is need for withdrawal or flight, since the danger is felt to be overwhelming. There are physical properties of anxiety. Adrenalin tends to be released from the medulla of the adrenal glands, which in turn produces acceleration of the heartbeat, as well as causing glycogen stored in the liver to be converted into sugar and released into the blood stream, thereby raising the immediate capability of the body for dealing with the sensed danger. These and other consequences of the action of the sympathetic division of the autonomic nervous system make anxiety a very real bodily condition.

Sometimes a distinction is made, as by Freud, between "real" and "neurotic" anxiety. Real anxiety, in this sense, is proportionate to an objective danger; whereas neurotic anxiety is entirely disproportionate to *external* threats, and is explicable only in terms of intrapsychic factors—as the threat posed by a repressed impulse which seeks to break into awareness. Both varieties of anxiety are involved in our discussion of self-realization, and we shall refer to both simply as "anxiety."

A distinction is sometimes made between "anxiety" and "fear," on the basis that fear requires a definite object of which one is afraid, whereas anxiety is not associated with such a consciously perceived object. Psychologists such as O. Hobart Mowrer and Rollo May have proposed that anxiety is "primal," occurring earlier in the emotional development of the individual; that fear is "derived" in the sense of being a more differentiated form of the emotion, having become attached through experience to discriminated object-threats of the outer world. In other words, this distinction would term "anxiety" a vague apprehension and uneasiness, whose cause one did not know; whereas similar feelings which might be experienced because, say, a large predatory animal was on the loose, would be termed "fear." While this distinction is highly useful for some purposes, we shall generally use the two terms, in our discussion, as synonymous, since such interchange will facilitate communication and will not generally introduce ambiguity.

So much for what anxiety is. Now for its effects upon us. These effects are, in brief—that *we seek to avoid it*. We seem to go to any length to escape anxiety, or to avoid feeling it. This becomes a basic issue in life for each of us, especially as regards *intense* anxiety.

Yet anxiety can be useful. A sprinkling of mild anxiety adds challenge and zest to life; without some sort of opposition to overcome, life would be dull indeed. Moreover, mild anxiety alerts the individual. It heralds more severe anxiety to follow, if proper defense is not instituted. It is therefore useful as an indicator of danger—of the necessity for starting defensive action—before the more severe threat, from within or from without, makes its actual appearance. Freud saw anxiety as serving the purposes of self-preservation, being a signal of the presence of some danger, an indicator that something is amiss in the life of the affected individual.

It has great biological utility, in that it "stirs up" the organism to emergency reaction. The visceral changes attending anxiety—increases in blood pressure and heart rate, secretion of adrenalin, and release of immediately available sugar from the liver—all contribute toward adaptive success in forceful physical activity, combat, or flight; it has strong drive properties, and strongly moves the individual to do something in order to bring about its reduction. In precisely these drive properties reside not only its value, but also its danger to self-realization.

Its *value* for self-realization is obvious and important. Each of us would be no more than a vegetable if we did not have real dangers and issues to face in life. What real meaning would there be in living if we did not face obstacles to the "good-life"? Through fighting "evil" in life—however each may define "evil" for himself—we realize the best that is in us. That is, we develop the vigor and sinews of our being through overcoming hazards and threats to ourselves and to our loved ones. In this sense, the anxieties and fears which herald real threats are catalysts for growth. They are the *sine qua non* of self-realization, and we are all indebted to them for the strength in our being: for the motives to grow, and for the battle-grounds on which each can meet inner adversity and move forward by surmounting it.

But—and this is a crucial point—anxiety may be so strong, or may last so long, that it may no longer exert a constructive influence. Instead, strong or persistent anxiety which exceeds the individual's capacity to tolerate it may exert a severely destructive influence upon his life. Such intense anxiety is deeply upsetting, saying to us in effect: "Your life is in disorder. . . . Your house is on fire. . . . You had better do something—quickly!"

But it does not identify the danger. It does not tell us where in the "house" the "fire" is actually located. And it does not indicate a course of action that would serve to deal with the danger. It only drives us blindly toward escape. Such alarm ringing can be extremely painful. It is likely to torment our waking hours, and to spill over into our sleep in the form of nightmares and insomnia.

The crux of the matter is this: In order to escape such anxiety, we may give up the opportunity to grow, and may instead cling desperately to any method at all that permits relief. When anxiety is strong enough or lasts long enough, we give up trying to realize ourselves, and the overriding urge in life becomes simply *escape* from anxiety. That anxiety is potentially useful then becomes an academic issue. The fact that escape from anxiety may be brought about through either of two significantly different pathways—through constructive, creative, self-advantageous modes enhancing self-realization on the one hand, or through self-destructive pathways on the other—loses its practical meaning in this instance. Such an intensely anxious person, one whose tolerance has been exceeded, no longer has the choice. He must instead grasp desperately at some mechanism for alleviating the anxiety level. He must allay the gnawing fear that is eating at his vitals. Some of these relief mechanisms may be severely self-defeating. Efficient in dulling the anxieties of life, they also may severely mortgage potentials for creative selfhood, both in the present and for many years to come.

What each of us is depends largely upon what each does with his anxiety, and his characteristic modes of handling it. The man is fortunate whose early years permitted him to develop constructive ways of dealing with his anxieties and fears. Non-creative methods may bleed off not only the anxieties, but also the opportunities to grow and realize oneself. Mechanisms for allaying anxiety may dissipate and block the raw materials of growth, its drives and energies, which might otherwise serve the achievement of a fuller measure of selfhood.

Let us now turn to an examination of some of these self-defeating ways of handling anxiety, and to see the sort of early home situations that lead one to such self-defeating mechanisms.

SECURITY THROUGH SELF-DEFEAT

The key to understanding much of the problem of self-defeat resides within the concept of "security operation." This term, coined by the psychiatrist Harry Stack Sullivan, denotes a sort of activity by which one finds relief from anxiety. The particular sort of activity Sullivan had in mind was this: The activity serves to lower anxiety by virtue of "maintaining a feeling of safety in the esteem reflected from the other person concerned."

For example, a child may learn that his parents approve when he works industriously at his lessons—working energetically may therefore evolve as a "security operation" for this particular child. He will tend to repeat this security operation, since we all seek to feel secure, and feel less anxious when significant persons think well of us—when we see a favorable appraisal of us reflected in their expressions.

Security operations are potentially useful. We could not possibly develop our minds fully if we did not have ways of lowering anxiety sufficiently to permit the flexible self-exploration so essential to growth. Of the mechanisms for lowering anxiety, those involving the implicit approval of others—the security operations—are of central importance in social life. But security operations, as we shall later see, may also constitute a powerful hindrance to personal and social progress.

Ordinarily, a child tends to develop properly and in a way assists self-realization through seeking to please his parent, for the healthy parent will approve of those activities which assist the child's development. But there are developmental situations which produce the reverse—which cause a child (and later adult)—to be self-defeating.

Each of us learns, in early experiences with significant persons, "when" to be anxious, and also "how much" anxiety will be mobilized. This learning of anxiety follows in large measure the laws of emotional conditioning. This sort of learning was first studied in the experimental laboratory by the Russian physiologist I. P. Pavlov, beginning at the turn of the century. The experimental design employed by Pavlov applies as well to human emotional conditioning: If two stimuli occur together, for example if a small quantity of meat is placed on the tongue at the same time as the ringing of a bell, and if these two stimuli are presented over and over again, then, in time, one stimulus will evoke the response formerly brought on by the other. Originally, in Pavlov's experiment, the taste of meat caused salivation; but in time, with the repeated pairing of the stimuli, the ringing of the bell alone caused salivation to occur.

Similarly, strong anxiety may be attached to situations which originally did not evoke such anxiety. For example, the child is naturally curious, and will move about to explore and learn; but if the parent "can't be bothered" with a child's roaming, she may so frighten him in discouraging his explorations that the very urge to explore and learn may become weighed down with a heavy burden of anxiety.

Through such conditioning, parents intentionally or otherwise create the inner emotional climate which follows the developing human for the rest of his life, for any way of behaving which permits anxiety avoidance or anxiety reduction tends to be repeated; and such "successful" repetition—successful in terms of anxiety reduction—tends to be "reinforced" even more. Thus, in time, those ways of behaving which help to reduce anxiety become important in themselves. That is, they become "security operations."

This is a helpful basis for educating the young. The loving and constructive parent will reinforce with his "appraisal" those activities of the child—those security operations—which are truly helpful toward self-realization. The parent's own attitudes in this way condition the direction in which the child will develop. But in considering these very same principles, we can see how the parent may unwittingly lead the child away from self-realization and toward self-defeat; with some parents, the very activities which would gain their approval might indeed be severely self-defeating regarding the individual's larger life-aims. In other words, the security operations whereby the child achieved a sense of acceptance by his parents may be the habits of reaction which seriously curtail his self-realization in later life. Certain qualities of the parent may operate in such a manner as to pervert the child's yearning for security into self-defeating outlets, since some people are inwardly driven to compete with *everyone*— including their own children. We could collectively term them "the competitive parent," and we shall see how they produce self-defeating offspring.

Let us note, in passing, that when we refer to "the unloving parent," "the competitive parent," "the power-oriented parent," and so on, throughout this book, we do not mean to imply that these are strictly different sorts of people. Actually, parents usually possess many of these qualities together; and the same parent may be unloving, competitive, and power-oriented. By the same token, when we describe motives which lead individuals to defeat themselves (hostility, power, guilt, etc.) we do not mean to say that any given individual defeats himself solely through one motive alone, for indeed many of these tend to operate together in the individual. But we must separate to some extent the qualities of the parent, and also the motives operating in the self-defeatist, to clarify our discussion.

The competitive parent must be ascendant in every situation. To maintain this position, he may enforce a cruel regimen. "When I spoke to my father," a self-defeating man recalled during therapy, "he would say I was wrong—that he alone was right. . . . So now," he said in a moment of insight, "I always anticipate being assaulted." He therefore tested me repeatedly: "I want to see whether you will try to castrate me, the way my father tried to do—whenever I told him anything." And he complained from time to time: "I feel pushed—as if you're always trying to prove that you're a better man than I am."

We looked into the question of what was "pushing" him, and found it was not I, but qualities of his parent that he had transferred to me. He recalled: "At home with my father—I had to make certain adjustments to even survive. . . . His rages—to me—were tremendously frightful . . . made me very afraid. . . . And now, when I think of it, I get a hot feeling in my chest—and I want to cry out!"

There was much to cry out about. Such a neurotically competitive parent pressures the child toward developing

self-defeating security operations; he will withhold com-
mendation when the child is truly constructive concerning
his maturing abilities and sensibilities, yet will beam approval when the child fits some parentally preconceived
notion of what the child's maturing self should be, however neurotically determined. And this preconceived notion, I need hardly add, exalts the parent's relative status,
however much it holds the child down to immature levels.

Some mothers, for example, insist on doing things for the
child—long after he is capable of doing such things for
himself. In one horrible example, a mother spoonfed her
son well into his eighth year; in another, a mother insisted
on doing all of her daughter's shopping even after the girl
had married and had a child of her own. These are obvious
and easily detected manifestations of neurotic competitiveness; the more discreet and covert facets of such parental influence may be even more destructive.

With such a parent, the child can find emotional security
—relative freedom from anxiety through acceptance by the
parent—only by undercutting his own self-realization regarding maturation. The security operations he will tend
to develop will therefore be of the self-defeating variety.
In the home of such a parent, the act of frank and open
success in moving ahead toward more truly mature behavior is often a cause of increased coldness in the parent.
The act of openly succeeding therefore, through conditioning, becomes a cue for anxiety and therefore tends to
be avoided.

Some of the child's best creative potentialities may thus
be discouraged by the neurotic or destructive parent, for
the child cannot tolerate the separation anxiety involved in
taking a stand at such an early age. He needs the parent's
favorable appraisal to hold in check agonizing inner feelings of loneliness and helplessness. If the child's outer

world were to be hostile, too, he would succumb to a deluge of anxiety. He therefore orients himself toward pleasing the competitive parent, rather than moving ahead just as quickly and effectively as he can. He may remain "cute" while he could be vigorous and "manly"; he may retain a "becoming" lisp, although his vocal apparatus is entirely ready for clear speech; he may exhibit childish emotional flamboyance and transparency, well knowing that his competitive parent lays exclusive claim to the reserve and artfulness required for social effectiveness.

Thus it comes to be that the child's repertoire of responses may be indeed efficient for meeting the ever present task of immediate anxiety reduction, yet may be altogether lacking for meeting success in the extra-familial world of society. The patterns of response which served quite adequately for getting along in the home, may be the very stumbling blocks which prevent success in the larger world of creative endeavor. Security operations developed over years of living with a neurotic authority figure may effectively destroy the individual's chances of relating adequately to future teachers and employers, and may preclude the possibility of relating to others and to his world in ways maximally advantageous to creative self-realization.

Suffering ostentatiously—"looking pitiful"—may be such a security operation. By appearing inept or ill, by undercutting his apparent dignity, the individual forestalls what he senses to be imminent attacks by others. "Look how wretched I am!" he had learned, was a cue for receiving parental acceptance; and he tends to repeat this operation when he is inwardly anxious, which may be continually.

This is one feature asociated with the concept of "masochism." The masochist welcomes pain, sensing that it defends him again social rejection, thereby defending him against experiencing anxiety and depression. One of the problems we meet in psychotherapy is related to this. The patient senses his suffering to be a defense against anxiety, a security operation; and he is loath to give up this inward successfully functioning—albeit self-defeating—defense.

An animal may be trained to *seek* pain, to appear to be a "masochist." The psychiatrist Jules H. Masserman and his co-worker Mary G. Jacques [1] clearly demonstrated this in laboratory experiments with cats in the following way: First, the investigators proved conclusively that electric shock and air blast are two unpleasant and traumatic sorts of stimulation for cats. Next, they gradually introduced air blast and electric shock *at the same time* as the cat achieved success in getting a pellet of food. In other words, they conditioned the cats to associating the blast and shock with the reduction of the hunger drive. The cats learned to operate an electric switch, which both released a pellet of food, and also subjected them to blast and shock. Thereafter the animals would squeeze through narrow passageways and surmount other obstacles to reach the switch, thus subjecting themselves to the painful experiences of blast and shock. Moreover, they would continue to do so when the food reward was given only occasionally, and even when it was withheld for several days.

Humans, also, will seek pain if the pain means the satisfaction of some essential need. Masserman's cats appeared to contradict the pleasure principle; they administered pain to themselves so as to satisfy hunger. The human masochist may seek humiliation and pain, may also appear to be violating this pleasure principle, so as to achieve emotional "security" through "acceptance"; and experiences with an essentially unloving and competitive parent may deeply reinforce the inner understanding that one is "accepted" only if one submits to derogation and humiliation.

Undue submissiveness may also constitute such an operation. Each of us deeply yearns to differentiate himself, as an independent and mature human being; yet, we are all ambivalent, for we also desire to be passive, dependent, and cared for. For the process of individuation—the separating of oneself from the herd— brings isolation and terrible feelings of loneliness and powerlessness. The maturation of individual reason and powers of mastery intrinsically incurs a severe cost in insecurity, doubt concerning one's values and roles, and anxiety over one's very significance in the world.

We all experience such insecurity when we embark upon some creative effort, some enterprise that will stamp us as "different." But for one reared by a competitive parent, these feelings can be excruciating. One man in therapy discovered it in this context: "Every time I try to use my own will I get a sort of heavy feeling. . . . And I get frightened."

From these unbearable feelings of isolation and loneliness, temporary relief may be had by giving up the urge toward separateness, the birthright of uniqueness, and accepting extreme conformity and submissiveness. By relinquishing the maturity and separateness of one's being, there is temporary relief from gnawing anxiety, the sense of being both alone and powerless, which we have all felt when daring to embark upon prolonged creative effort. Needless to say, the employment of this security operation brings to an end all effective work on the enterprise.

The neurotically competitive parent increases the likelihood of the continued utilization of this security operation by the developing child and later adult. For when the child appears reasonably self-reliant, he sometimes sees a cloud of suspicion and largely unconscious resentment in the parent's expression and reactions. To be an accepted child, he must be a relatively dependent child. As one man who had been dominated by his mother up through his married years came to see it: "I *want* to develop my own power to function . . . . But I am afraid that if I show I can get on alone—I will lose my mother's affection."

While it is true that this sort of parent desires the child to be sufficiently effectual so as to permit proud display to the world as an extension of her own ego, yet there is the conflicting desire that the parent alone be intelligent and capable in the household. The result of this conflict is often a merciless goading of the child toward unattainable heights of accomplishment, an outward rejection of the child for not meeting these actually impossible levels of attainment, and an inner resentment over the child's *actual* accomplishments and level of maturation. There is perfectionism in the context of certain failure, and nihilism toward areas of probable success.

Such a child becomes neurotically anxious over signs of emerging capabilities and uniqueness. Impelled by his anxiety and wish for acceptance toward the never-never land of perfection, and repelled from the dangerous possibilities of actual—though mundane—accomplishment, his solution to this dilemma is often abject dependence and submissiveness. By giving up his will, by self-infantilization, he finds escape at least from parental rejection because of the competition implicit in maturation; although he is bound, in any event, to be disparaged and scorned for ineffectuality, fancied or real. Through yielding his initiative and integrity, submerging his volition and mental processes within another person, and assuming a passive-receptive relation to a larger and apparently stronger individual, he can participate in the will of the larger person, and sense a primitive omnipotence through this annihilation of selfhood.

This makes for excessive dependence, for an inability

to think for oneself and to carry out plans to their ultimate fulfillment, and for a clinging to the reason and judgment of others, to those who may actually be less capable of reaching valid judgments than he. Strangely enough, it is the intensely hostile and rejecting parent who produces the clinging adult: For the continually tense and anxious child fears to assert his developing powers lest such independence jeopardize whatever shred of acceptance he now receives from the dominating parents. He remains infantilized, dependent, and lastingly anxious. As an adult he may possess strong innate intellectual potentials, yet he may display a strikingly bizarre inability to do anything by himself.

In our neurotic culture, undercutting one's creativity can allay anxiety. There is always room for the "regular fellow," the one who accepts cultural fictions and prejudices without question. But the independent one finds the going considerably more difficult. Granted the many *inner* blessings which accrue to the creative way of life, yet, rejection by the group—to greater or lesser extents—is often a consequence of conscientious adherence to independent thought.

For there is separateness, individuality, alone-ness in creating, and one fears that the protracted creative effort may all be an embarrassing or even tragic error, that it may be foolish to spend so much time on the venture, that a wiser man might have taken the old well-beaten path. Whereas in conformity there is predictability of outcome and relative safety rather than this ominous void of the unknown. Of course, the self's possibilities can only be realized through hazarding the unknown, through exposing oneself to new modes of dealing with life; yet there is danger in this newness, and there is therefore fear and anxiety.

The neurotic competitiveness which infects our time adds to the anxiety of creating. The child must hazard rejection by the domineering parent who inwardly seeks to infantilize; the young professional in his green and productive years must share his creative thinking in an atmosphere which rewards narrow intellectual partisanship. Small wonder that a gifted but minimally productive artist literally experienced a cold sweat when he began a project: "It is as if I am in a trench, and have to go over the top with a bayonet."

This anticipation of envy is transferred to the world outside the home. This is not to say that the world of reality, in our time, does not in fact call for ample evidence of mediocrity, for getting along with the herd. If it is stylish to shuffle in lock step, the man who walks independently soon learns the sting of begrudging envy and projected self-hatred. "Playing ball," being a member of a "team," are the desiderata to which the compulsive socializers refer to justify disparaging and abusing the creative individual who chooses to walk alone. But above and beyond the gadfly nuisances which emerge from the herd, the self-defeatist fears creative success, lest the envy of others drive him to ruin.

However disastrous such compulsive conformity and submissiveness may be to the creative life, it is palpably true that it stifles anxiety. Though its defensive effect is only temporary, and though it may in the long run create more problems than it solves, such defense does work, and serves as a way of alleviating the immediate tension of anxiety.

This being so, the individual may suffer severe inhibition when he seeks to assert his will, to make decisions, and to act upon them. For he has become habituated to coping with anxiety by turning away from self-assertion. Compulsive submissiveness is a safety device; and efforts to drop the device, and to alter the indiscriminate dependence upon another, will touch off deep and intense anxiety.

The man who had been spoonfed until the age of eight made a determined effort to assert himself, and reported, "Anything I do for myself, that *helps* me—makes me feel anxious. . . . But when I goof off—I *don't* feel anxious." And he came to the logical conclusion: "I guess I'm afraid to exercise the power that is mine to exert." In time, the man's own self-assertiveness was freed, and it took the form of competing with me during sessions. I pointed this out, and he said "It's terrible! . . . The mere *seeing* of 'competitiveness' frightens me—makes me feel I am *bad*!" And he added, some time later: "It seems that if I compete— I must do so in ways which are not perceptible—to either you or to me," which was true enough of his actions in the family milieu in which he was reared, and explains, in part, why his efforts at self-assertion has been so crude and so "blind."

The inhibition of one's ability to function often serves to avoid anxiety-producing situations or activities. It follows, therefore, that such a compulsively clinging individual may suffer fatigue and other signs of inhibition when he makes a stab at self-assertion. Such inhibition of self-assertion may occur on many levels. The more superficial inhibitions may curtail one's freedom to act upon one's wishes, or even to ask for something which is in one's own interest. But the deeper and more devastating inhibitions effect the inner processes themselves, so that one can not even know clearly what one wants or thinks.

Anxiety is indeed avoided by such self-defeating mechanisms, but at the price of creativity. For anxiety is an alarm signal whose proper observance can lead to new and useful discoveries of truth and human potentials. The opiate of self-defeat circumvents immediate anxiety, but excludes opportunities for exploration and growth. These defensive attitudes toward success may have once possessed valid meaning for self-preservation. In the early home, such self-defeatism had served as a way of maintaining the integrity and survival of selfhood under most severe and trying conditions. The façade of ineptness had deflected parental attack during the years when even nominal acceptance was vitally needed. But in the larger world of creative opportunity, the adult may continue his self-defeatism for the purpose of avoiding anxiety. And for the adult, these self-defeating techniques do *not* possess defensive validity in the world of reality, but are only enormously self-destructive. Thus, the method of defending oneself against anxiety may be a far more serious threat to self-realization than was the original danger.

NOTES

[1] Jules H. Masserman and Mary Grier Jacques, "Experimental Masochism" in *Archives of Neurology and Psychiatry*, Vol. 60 (1948), pp. 402–404.

IV

PITFALLS OF POWER

Pyrrhus, king of Epirus twenty-two centuries ago, found himself continually embroiled in wars. The victories he won were many; but he is reported by Plutarch to have remarked after one costly battle that another such victory "would utterly undo him." In the end, he was killed in a street skirmish.

Many of us, similarly, go through life winning "victories" which cost dearly in terms of time and effort, and which yield no long-term satisfactions. We become involved in struggles which serve no one; we dissipate our energies in empty causes; we permit our urge toward self-realization to be ensnared by false objectives. We, too, experience our "Pyrrhic victories"; and these often add up to a life of resounding self-defeat.

A key to this waste of human creative potential resides in the overly urgent striving for a sense of individual power. It was this craving for prestige and dominance which Alfred Adler termed the "most prominent evil of our civilization." And though it be prominent, we are reluctant to perceive it; we attribute to many sorts of more acceptable motives—love, altruism, rational self-interest—what is far more likely to be the influence of a neurotic hunger for power.

This may seem strange, since—is not the elevated sense of competence an essential feature of self-realization? And is not the striving for power in order to deal effectively with one's life space at the very heart of seeking to grow?

Indeed they are. But by the "striving for power," as we employ the term, we do not mean the realistic and mature desire for competence and reasonable self-sufficiency which Harry Stack Sullivan termed the "power motive." We mean, rather, an immature craving for omnipotence, a nebulous hunger for unlimited power over all others in the universe, which in Sullivan's terminology is the "power drive," the sort of diffuse and ill-modulated pressure toward self-assertion characterizing what Freudian psychoanalysts term the "anal character." It does not lead to realistic satisfaction through achievement; rather, the neurotic striving for power is a snare which destroys true creativity and actively undermines the valid achievement of selfhood. This neurotic striving for power differs from the healthful wish for competence in the following two respects: As to degree, this wish for power is unlimited, and is essentially a primitive reaching for omnipotence; and as to direction, the neurotic quest aims at power for the sake of power *alone*, rather than for the increased capacity to serve some living thing.

Occurrences often met with in mental hospitals reveal that the weakest of mortals most crave immoderate power. The psychotic who has lost all his worldly possessions and skills, including reason itself, stands motionless, making a sign at the sun. This posture and this sign constitute his armamentarium for controlling vast forces, including the sun itself. The often met delusions of the insane frequently serve this purpose of providing vast power to outweigh and overbalance inwardly sensed powerlessness and desolation.

The bizarre power maneuvers and delusions of the insane are obvious. But many of us, without awareness, can also be entrapped in the snares of a neurotic quest for power. Though we still retain our reason, we may nonetheless pay tribute to habitual power operations which sap the energies and seriously undercut the process of self-realization. Let us therefore carefully examine this inordinate urge to power.

FATEFUL ALTERNATIVES

The urge to power derives its essential meaning from this: *It is a mode of defending oneself against anxiety.* This defensive role of power is at the crux of our entire discussion, and provides a basis for understanding the following paradox: In order to experience an unrealistic sense of power, a man will often undermine and destroy his valid potentials for realistic competence and achievement.

Karen Horney is pre-eminent in the study of this area. Although the self-defeating potential of power seeking had been recognized from at least the time of Isaiah onward, and was insightfully structured by Nietzsche, it was Horney who most fully developed its implications for self-realization.

Within a social milieu, Horney tells us, there are two basic ways of defending oneself from anxiety: 1) through the sense of sharing in a love relationship, and 2) through the sense of individual power. This dichotomy of defenses, as we shall see, has tremendous bearing upon personal freedom for exploring and achieving the fullest limits of creative selfhood. One defense is that of mutualism, of partaking of the larger life, of living *with* others. The second is that of individual power, of separating the "good" of one's own life from the "good" of others, of relatively narrow self-interest.[1]

Horney terms one defense "securing affection"; here the motto is: "If you love me you will not hurt me." The other is "power," and here the motto is: "If I have power, no one can hurt me." The latter is similar to Sullivan's conception that one of the basic elements in the feeling of security is the belief that one has sufficient power in an interpersonal situation, that one can feel "in control" of the situation.

Defense through love and defense through power, Horney teaches, have an important inverse functional relationship. That is, where the sense of being loved functions well, there is less need for the sense of individual power; and conversely, where one feels unloved, there is an intense craving for power.

The wish for power has deep roots. It manifests itself very early in the life of every child. One perceptive mother's comment, "Sometimes I get the feeling that my baby is trying to outsmart me!" is valid for some period in every child's life. The infant reaches for the moon, Sullivan tells us; and every young human must outgrow an obvious thirst for omnipotence.

If we all crave omnipotence in infancy and childhood, one might ask, then how do we ever come to give up this glittering bauble of unlimited power? And the answer is, in a word, *love*. The affection, the sense of security a child receives through his parents' warm feelings for him so bind his anxiety that he need not cling to primitive omnipotence fantasies in self-defense. Instead, being relatively anxiety-free, he can satisfy his natural curiosity and look openly upon the real world of facts and phenomena. Moreover, the affectionate parents will make known their wishes. The child is asked to eat on time, to respond to sounds, and gradually to control his elimination. These are requests that face up to reality. Each represents an inroad upon the child's "omnipotent" will; but when he is shown sufficient warmth, the child, fairly willingly, gives up the role of the potentially omnipotent tyrant (although some reluctance is bound to be experienced, and some rebellion will always be met).

Early experiences determine the degree of success achieved in this yielding of the wish for omnipotence, this assumption of social cooperation. Where the parents are duly warm and affectionate, this transition is relatively smooth. But where parents are essentially disinterested and egotistical, the child is denied the defense through love, and therefore clings tenaciously to the primitive will to power.

Negativism in some degree is quite normal in children. Some resistive behavior is clearly discernible during the first few months of the infant's life. But normal personality development, that which augurs well for adult self-realization, requires the gradual substitution of cooperative defenses for those of power operations. By the time the child is four or so, he should be reasonably cooperative.

Where personal significance is not bolstered by the larger life of reasonable love and mutualism, the child clings to negativism and power. Where he feels that he will not be given the signs of warmth and acceptance he so vitally needs he will tend to seize things for himself, to steal. If cooperating does not bind anxiety, he will tend to retain individual power and negation as defenses and supports of his significance. Sullivan said it this way: "If mother says 'It's time for little Willie to go to bed' and little Willie goes; that is one thing. . . . If now, instead of going to bed, little Willie says 'No' and reinforces his non-cooperation with all means at his disposal, his significance in his world may become at least briefly, very great."

Love is a simple thing which avoids complex difficulties. Steering a middle course between over-restraint and under-discipline is one consequence of genuine parental warmth. Where the parents are overly restrictive and interfere unnecessarily with the child's valid prerogatives and activities, his hostility and negativism are more likely to be reinforced. Or, at the other extreme, where they do not take a sufficiently firm stand to enforce *their* own proper prerogatives, where they permit the child to control the entire family by his temper tantrums, where they "spoil" the child by yielding and rewarding him for the display of unreasonable willfulness—there the child will be reluctant to yield to inner omnipotence fantasies and make his peace with reality. Both extremes tend to be avoided by the existence of true affection in the parent, and by the application of ordinary common sense. Where the parent does not habitually use such sense in dealing with the child, we have reason to question the nature of his feelings.

We often find the parent who alternates between over-severity and spoiling, between unrealistic verbal supervaluation of the child and disparaging and shaming him. The cause is generally a lack of genuine affection in the parent; in its stead are found the inner alternation of hostility and guilt, a sequence which explains the outer alternation between lionizing the child as a rediscovered favorite toy, and humiliating him as a necessary but much resented evil. The child's resulting self-concept and self-esteem are accordingly chaotic, and his infantilizing reluctance to yield primitive power operations is therefore understandable on the basis of defensive needs.

Our culture contributes to the supervaluation of individual power, a thesis which has been fully developed by such psychoanalysts as Franz Alexander and Karen Horney. For the "basic evil" in our culture, Horney tells us, is a lack of genuine warmth and affection; and this, as we have developed, leads to a much-increased urge to individual power. Anthropologists, such as Ruth Benedict, have shown a very different situation to exist in less competitive cultures, where emotional security is not as closely linked with individual status. Among the Pueblo Indians of New Mexico, for example, where childhood is associated with much love and kindness, individual prowess and power are severely scorned, and admiration given to ready social cooperation.

Power possesses intrinsic value as a defense against anxiety. We have all learned from personal experience that physical pain, or trial, or deprivation of some sort is much easier to bear if one knows that one can terminate it at will. Powerlessness in the face of distress adds considerably to the pain of that distress.

Healthy maturation involves the gradual modification of mastery behavior in the light of reason. Such transition of power techniques along the developmental scale passes from the random crying, slashing, and omnipotence fantasies of the infant through the protracted realistic reasoning and long term purposeful effort of the healthy creative adult. Adult maturity normally includes wholesome patterns by which we can achieve a realistic sense of considerable power, prestige, and mastery over our environment.

But the power and mastery maneuvers which we are

about to discuss, the snares of power which trap the self's creative potentials—these involve a compulsive need to dominate others; and this need is expressed rigidly, without regard to whether or not such need to dominate is realistic. We deal with the unrealistic craving for power as a *character* trait, as a habitual approach to life and its activities, one which takes its cue largely from within the individual, rather than from the outer life-situation in which he finds himself. This sort of power orientation makes for a peculiar contrast: Feelings of omnipotence and powerlessness exist side by side. As one intelligent young executive perceived it: "On the one hand I feel so strong that no one could touch me; and yet, on the other hand, I feel so vulnerable—that anyone could utterly destroy me!"

Let us turn now to the many ways in which the overly urgent craving for individual power curtails *true* power and capability, and examine how the blind quest for power causes serious inroads upon the inner freedom for self-realization.

POWER AND SELF-REALIZATION

One might imagine that an unbridled craving for individual power would further productive creativity. But many varieties of considerations indicate the reverse to be true: that the power orientation undercuts our freedom for successful achievement, and actually dissipates and perverts the potentially constructive energies of self.

The power orientation, as we have seen, stems from a primitive level of personality organization. It is apt, therefore, to be stamped with the central wish of this primitive level, *omnipotence*. It tends to ignore the limitations imposed by reality, and to "reach for the moon" in creative effort. There are unfortunate facets of the functional inter-relationship between level of aspiration and actual achievement. Compulsive reaching for the moon is hardly likely to result in the successful grasp of anything celestial; it is more likely to result in discouragement and the cessation of purposeful reaching altogether. Neurotic perfectionism is thus consonant with the power orientation. And perfectionism is self-defeating by definition, for it defines the goal as the unattainable. It is characterized by what Freudians term "narcissism"; and narcissistic personalities are notoriously underachieving in the world of reality.

Such perfectionism takes the place of realistic attainment. For when nothing short of perfect is acceptable, the achievement of merely superior results precipitates feelings of worthlessness and depression. When actual achievement is thus a cue for such frustration and sadness, it tends to be avoided. Thus, perfectionism tends to coexist with unproductiveness.

The existence of perfectionism is consistent with the individual's life history. Where the parent perceives the child to be but an appendage of his own power-oriented self, the parent will demand perfection from the child, just as he does from himself. Such overly rigorous parental standards tend to be introjected by the child, and come to be part of his own inner values. Since the early power-oriented parent—and later one's own derived standards of perfectionism—will criticize and disparage whatever one produces, there is intense inner pressure toward rendering every achievement flawless, impervious to the impending attack. Consequently, it is the more necessary to seek to maintain a grandiose conception of one's capabilities, in order to avoid both the anxiety over rejection by others, and that which ensues from contempt for self.

One highly gifted artist whose father had opposed her

developing talents at every turn defended herself from the barrage of depression that his derogation repeatedly unloosed with this inner hope: "I had the feeling that I would not only *paint*—but I would paint in an entirely new color —that no one else had ever mixed!" So she ruined and discarded excellent paintings close to completion. They were not "good enough." "I despise myself!" she came eventually to say, and validly. But the next day she was back to feelings of grandiosity, of inwardly feeling a "great painting" would yet result—one "great" enough to silence forever her hateful and perfectionist father.

Such inner grandiosity is malignantly self-perpetuating. A vicious circle comes into existence, in which perfection is sought to counterbalance underlying feelings of worthlessness; and since the search for perfection precludes all possibility of gratification, such feelings of worthlessness are reinforced by actual repeated failures. A grandiose conception of self works therefore toward undercutting the stature of the actualized self.

This is illustrated by the remark of a self-defeatist: "I seem to want to have the feeling that I'm best in *everything;* and if I'm not best in everything—then I'm *nothing!*" It is consequently not difficult to grasp the meaning of this man's need to procrastinate. He feared putting himself to the test of action, for he would find his performance to be less than perfect, and this would re-arouse dreaded underlying feelings of worthlessness and insignificance.

The infant's situation is this: omnipotence in fantasy; powerlessness in reality. This omnipotence-powerlessness constellation persists in the power orientation, and is expressed in perfectionism. It constitutes a dangerous situation for mental health, for a defense against anxiety is found in a compulsive striving after absolute supremacy, and yet stark ineffectuality exists in reality.

One resulting pattern which undermines creativity is that the power-oriented individual may deal with anxiety by tearing up, or otherwise destroying, what he has completed and "starting over" again. This destruction of partially completed work does not result from a critical appraisal; it rather occurs habitually and irrationally.

This can go on time and again, until a writer, over the years, may produce little more than half-finished manuscripts and many wastepaper baskets full of earlier efforts. Or a gifted artist may dawdle for years, and never quite get together a portfolio or exhibit through which he could present his talent to the world. The net result is the maintenance of a grandiose conception of one's ability: For if nothing is completed, then one's ability cannot be tested, judged, or found wanting.

Another pattern serving the same purpose is this: Such perfectionists avoid permitting themselves full opportunity to show their true ability. If they do complete and submit a creative assignment, they let it be known that it was completed under extreme conditions of pressure, of time, fatigue, inadequate materials. In this way they manage to achieve sufficiently to get along in life, yet avoid putting their abilities and grandiose self-concept to a definitive test. A specific stratagem often employed for this purpose is to let months go by without doing a stitch of work on a deadline assignment, and then to stay awake for days on end in order to complete it in a flurry of frenzied effort. The completion thus becomes a triumph in itself, that is, that it was able to get done at all, when time had grown so short. Out of certain defeat, which would have been met if they had put their grandiose inner self-concept to the test of total effort, such neurotic power-oriented persons pull victory; and out of such repeated victories is born hack-mediocrity, where there could have been truly valuable, albeit non-perfect, achievement.

Similarly, perfectionism causes one to turn away from real and immediate opportunities for the completion of a creative task. When a vacation comes due, and several weeks of time are at hand, the perfectionist will often find non-essential or senseless chores which consume the vacation time, and prevent putting his talent to the test of actual accomplishment. "I wanted a reason to keep me from my painting," admitted such an artist in a moment of insight, after a vacation wasted in this manner. "I somehow felt a great deal of fear—every time I mixed my paints. . . . I had a feeling like being on the stage."

The power-oriented, since perfectionistic, cannot tolerate the disclosure of any shortcoming or weakness. He is unduly humiliated by such disclosures about the self, and therefore inwardly seeks to prevent self-knowledge.

The thirst for perfection, and the reluctance to perceive imperfections intrinsic to self obviously hamper constructive effort in psychotherapy. An early psychoanalyst, Karl Abraham, described the difficulties met by such people when they attempt to succeed at psychotherapy: "They only say things which are ego-syntonic. These patients are particularly sensitive to anything which injures their self-love. They are inclined to feel humiliated by every fact that is established in their psychoanalysis, and they are continually on guard against suffering such humiliation."

This resistance against self-knowledge severely undercuts creative potential. For the rich hinterland of creative ideas resides deep within the self, and the inner inhibition to free access to this fertile source of personal genius impoverishes personal powers. Formal logic does indeed contribute largely to the conscious processes of intellectualization; but the contributions of the unconscious to hypotheses essential to imaginative creation —often referred to as "intuition"—are many and weighty. Whoever does not possess relatively free access to the "mindedness" lying beneath formal logic is at a serious disadvantage in creative effort. Deep within our selves are untried qualities of selfhood; and whoever habitually turns from self-knowledge deprives himself of these essential cues and opportunities for self-realization.

One facet of the reluctance to face oneself is the inability to employ constructive criticism advantageously. As Alfred Adler saw it, such power-oriented people "disregard anything originating in another human being," and react to every suggestion as an insult. In spite of their desire to make the most of ideas at hand, and although they pride themselves on openness and reasonableness, their need to be correct and dominant is so intense that, again quoting Adler, "They actually say 'no!' when they want to say 'yes!'"

Any criticism, however constructive, threatens the perfectionistic person deeply, and thereby unleashes further hostility, which adds further to his difficulties. By way of defense, he clings more tenaciously to a grandiose conception of himself—termed the "glorified self" by Horney, and the "superiority complex" by Adler. This arrogation to a self-concept of enormous power is born not of actual strength, but of a gnawing sense of weakness. It covers over the sorts of inner understanding termed by Adler the "inferiority complex."

This emphasis upon pride, this seeking for absolute perfection, this reluctance to perceive oneself as being a human with defects intrinsic to mankind, all contribute toward the building of a false conception of self, thus making for increasing difficulty in facing oneself, and for increasing alienation from the world.

One man entered treatment because he was awakened night after night in terror by a repetitive nightmare. He said, "I have the feeling I'm shrinking. . . . I have the sensations as if I keep getting smaller and smaller!" He was, on the surface, a cocksure, blustering man. Though he had gone only as far as completing high school, he told me, with finality, that there was *nothing* he could not learn. When I asked, "Nuclear physics, too?" he maintained a strained cordiality, and took my question lightly. It was all sham, and he knew it. But he did not *want* to know it. He psychologically barricaded himself against accepting his human limitations. Yet his excruciating dreams of shrinking smaller and smaller, until there was practically nothing left, led him to explore his true inner world. He descended gradually to unbearable feelings of inadequacy, and shaken, he asked: "Which is the *real* me?" He found, eventually, that it was neither the arrogant possessor of omnipotence, nor the timid man drowning in a sea of insignificance. He was in reality quite a likable and potentially highly effectual person with limitations and definite strengths. But such humanness had not been enough. "I withdrew into fantasy," he came eventually to see, "because I could not accept who I really was." Perfectionism had served as an opiate, and alienation from himself had been an inescapable consequence.

Such alienation materially lessens the intimate contact which one continually makes with inner feelings and understandings. It impairs the ability to perceive honestly the tensions and emotions intrinsic to one's own experience, and makes for empty formalism in art and hackneyed pedantry in the social sciences: For fully original thought and expression are not obtainable through formal logic alone—one must walk humbly to one's inner heart, and listen there in childlike candor.

Educability also falls prey to power, for psychological growth and education are based upon the search for adequacy. They are a response to anxiety, to the sense of what Adler terms "weakness," and Horney calls a "need to change." But a power orientation defeats this process on two grounds: It resists perceiving whatever requires change —for this is a weakness and an insult to a perfectionistic self-concept—and it quickly binds anxiety with a power maneuver, rather than utilizing the energy displacement for self-exploration and growth.

It curtails the ability to see truth. The grandiose inner conception of self is rigidly maintained at the expense of clear perception; events are distorted so as to remove threats to such a self-concept. Sullivan phrased it pointedly: "To the extent that one is preoccupied with those power operations . . . one's foresight is useless. . . . One foresees trains of events in which all the people concerned are . . . illusions, including the mighty magician himself." An engineer in treatment perceived it in this light: "I was so obsessed with the fixed need to be a genius, that I could never face my fears and anxieties about taking tests—or even about living life. . . . I couldn't be a human, and experience my fears—like everybody else."

The ability to work with others is impaired. A research chemist, for example, resisted accepting a supervisor's suggestions. It developed that these suggestions were excellent, but were rejected solely because of the chemist's need to consider himself as a completely independent and all powerful thinker. Similarly, a writer put a fairly good manuscript on the shelf and let it gather dust after it had been rejected by only one publisher. Rejections of this sort, which are part and parcel of the writer's life, were for him agonizing assaults upon his grandiose self-concept.

The power orientation and its grandiose inner self-concept corrupt regard for one's truest interests, and put pride in their stead. Such an orientation increases susceptibility to flattery. The overly hungry are not inclined to be discerning. When men behave like fools, it is usually to sustain a cherished concept of what one's ego is supposed to be.

It also undermines realistic aspiration. Where biological needs and appetites guide goals and objectives, the wisdom of the body is always present. But where the craving for power is uppermost, such wisdom is lacking, and one may crave wordly goods without end and without hope of real satisfaction. In Biblical terms: "He that loveth silver shall not be satisfied with silver; nor he that loveth abundance with increase...." A power orientation may cause people to jump artificial hurdles in life. The procurement and conspicuous spending of money is one such artificiality, and mainly serves pride at the expense of other more creative aspects of life. But it is not alone the attainment of money which saps our energies. Many kinds of empty activities may be pursued, simply to bolster the sense of pride and power. One bright young man, for example, repeatedly undertook a fairly unpleasant task which he knew how to do unusually quickly, thereby feeling he was impressing others by doing it. But the task consumed his time and energy, without really serving himself or any other living thing.

Valid needs are relegated to positions of lesser importance because of power cravings. In therapy, for example, the need to improve is sometimes displaced by the urge to be powerful; and as Karl Abraham reported, power-oriented people tend to bring the analysis under the control of the "pleasure principle"; that is, they use time during therapy sessions for achieving narcissistic gratification, for bolstering the sense of personal power, rather than for moving ahead. They actually bristle when the therapist makes what appears to be a "brilliant" interpretation; and as Horney pointed out so perceptively, the therapist's interpretation does not even have to be correct to produce this effect, but only needs to *appear* to be brilliant.

The power-oriented individual may turn away from what he truly wants and needs, so as to thwart authority, or demonstrate his independence; he may withdraw, temporarily or permanently, from personal contacts which promise gratification, for needing or depending upon someone insults his pride.

While posing as a mature adult, he remains essentially childish. Maturity is not reached until one seeks primarily to satisfy one's own valid inner standards; whereas the pride-ridden is often preoccupied with what others think about him, and with the impression he makes. Yet, though he be overly concerned with what others think of him, he finds it repugnant to cooperate with them; he is still immersed in his little world of parent-child interaction, and remains essentially a "naughty child" who plays at being an adult. One such young man spent a small fortune decorating a one and a half room apartment with antiques. Since space was limited, he literally filled his father's garage with the overflow of furniture and paintings. The point of it all was, of course, conspicuous consumption. He did not lose many opportunities to tell visitors about that garage and its decaying contents.

Overemphasis upon pride and power restrict the ability to give of oneself; and freedom to give of that which is within is essential for the creative unfolding of selfhood. In therapy, such people find great difficulty in producing free associations; in the world outside the clinic, they tend to be rigidly inhibited: For the world within, however rich and fertile it may be, yet contains impulses and elements which bar perfection or the maintenance of a grandiose self-concept—*ergo*, the reluctance to face oneself broadly and freely. In situations calling for warmth and wide emotional responsiveness, the power-oriented will tend therefore to be emotionally flat or stereotyped.

The craving for unlimited power undermines the freedom to apply oneself to a task, or to persevere at it. For the meaning of the creative task assumes vicious proportions to the one who inwardly wants to assume all the power in the world. Applying oneself, to such a power-oriented person, is therefore a signal for severe anxiety: For the inner meaning of personal effort is well appreciated deep within one's being, and one's emotions reflect such inner understanding. To one who harbors infantile omnipotence wishes and anticipations, the wielding of power and the exercising of will are dangerous and severely frightening. I asked one of them why this was so, and he replied: "The first thing that comes to mind is—'I'll overwhelm the world!'" Then he related a dream: "On the way home, at twilight, filled with resentment against the townspeople, I decided to fly—a trick which I had kept secret. . . . I ran, leaped into the air, but could scarcely rise. Angry, determined to prove to myself that I had the will and power to fly, I tried again—and was successful this time. I soared at a great height and was exhilarated."

But there was a second part to this dream: "When I returned home and entered the house, I heard a strange singing, a weird kind of melody, like an incantation—coming from a deserted room. It chilled me. Picking up a poker from the fireplace, I went toward the room. . . . It was crowded with people . . . soberly dressed. I knew they were there for a sinister purpose and that they were not real. I swung the poker through the air, and it passed through their bodies—proving what I suspected. There was one man among them, however, who was tall, imposing, and with a stern face. I approached him fearfully and swung the poker at his head. The poker struck him a sharp blow, but he never flinched, and continued to stare at me. 'Only Satan,' I said to myself, 'could be real, and this man, therefore, was Satan.' I called him by his name. . . . He smiled grimly—and then I awoke from my dream."

The dream describes well the sort of "sinister" tide such a man must swim against in seeking to create. His deep anxiety over asserting himself—and he was, incidentally, endowed with intellectual brilliance—manifested itself in this ghoulish nightmare, with its two phases, and which taught this lesson: "If you assert your very considerable personal power—cloaked as it is by resentment and omnipotence—you will pay for it!" In his waking life, he habitually avoided such "payment" by simply not "flying," that is, by backing away from the full employment of his creative talent and by remaining instead what was for him—a dwarfish mediocrity.

To such a person, life's alternatives are between "omnipotence" and "slavery," depending upon whether he or someone else has the upper hand. Coming late to a therapy session therefore unleashes tremendous anxiety, for the clash of wills is sensed—even in this petty instance—to involve forces of enormous magnitude.

Horney sees a "vicious circle" developing out of the neurotic striving for power. Somewhat simplified, her view is this: A basic insecurity drives the individual toward the excessive craving for power; and this excessive urge to power—along with its neurotic competitiveness—contributes further to anxiety, actual failure, and further insecurity. Thus, the circle is begun again.

To be free to succeed, one must be free to fail, for creative effort always occurs within the context of possible failure. But the power-oriented person cannot permit himself the inner stress of honest failure. To a personality organization so crucially hinged upon an inner sense of omnipotence failure is catastrophic, and its perception is unbearable. Since his need for mastery is compulsive, he will tend to avoid challenges to his creative potential. Although highly endowed with strength and intelligence, he tends to recoil from meeting the test of life, from taking risks in seeking the fullest realization of interaction between potentials for creating and opportunities afforded by his world. While appearing to possess courage within the confines of established social interaction, he inwardly cringes when facing new ideas and new possibilities. For the new is the uncertain; the uncertain implies risk to mastery; and risks to mastery are fraught with fear for one whose significance rests upon individual power.

Alfred Adler has fully described the defensive "alibis" which undercut the creativity of the power-oriented. They avoid the test of their powers and do not permit themselves a full chance to create; rather, they carry a "life preserver" at all times—a ready explanation of why they never had an opportunity to show what they really could do.

Some set forth impossible conditions, which must be met before they will fully cooperate with society, before they will throw their full talents onto the scales. Others avoid the main arena of creativity—the area in which they possess truly outstanding talent—and confine their energy outlets to some "side show" of life, where their talents are not called upon. They may stress some minor congenital defect, implying that they cannot commit themselves to full effort because of it; or they may languish over making decisions until opportunities are past. A creative task may be approached without proper preparation, without leaving enough time to do it adequately, or without industrious application; the net effect being that although such a person's achievement falls far short of his potential, yet—in the words of Adler—"He becomes, so to speak, a double hero who has done with one hand what others can only do with two hands!"

One of the costs of such neurotic perfectionism was curiously illustrated by the student who had to be the first to complete every examination. "Heavens knows how much I lost," he reflected in later years, "through having to walk out *first* this way, from every examination room."

Some degree of passivity is required for optimal creativity. One must relax, one must become temporarily passive-receptive, one must permit a temporary regression to a less masterful role, one must experience the primitive and irrational, if fullest contact is to be made with that rich reservoir of creative ideas which lies close to the unconscious. But this passivity is inconsistent with the strict intellectual control that the power orientation demands, and creativity suffers. Such an individual often finds it difficult to apply himself methodically to a task, since there is little glory in conscientious work-habits; there is, rather, insult to pride. He welcomes the generalization and drama which surround early phases of creative enterprise, but is deeply offended by the painstaking labor generally required for its completion. His are the many projects born in high hope and aborted through what appears to be indolence yet is, in reality, defensive defection from methodical self-application. He craves achievement without effort, and superiority without the risk of being occasionally inferior. He sits down at a typewriter to compose great literature without preparatory notes, and to effect complex creative processes simultaneously. That the associative and critical aspects of creative effort require different moods and approaches is not palatable to him; he must combine them all and overcome all obstacles in one grandiose flourish. And when the choice inwardly presents itself between a pose of effortless superiority devoid of accomplishment, and methodical self-application, leading gradually to creative achievement, his inner defensive needs are so urgent that he clings compulsively to the former.

Few tyrannies so corrupt and pervert the creative unfolding of the self's potentials as that exercised by perfectionism. It renders the slightest creative task fraught with anxiety, and places the creator under intense fear of failure, since his sense of personal significance hangs continually in the balance. And since the perfect is obviously the unattainable, he continually experiences a deeply corrupting condition—the seeking of inner peace through attempting to satisfy standards which are by definition insatiable. While his few actual achievements may truly be highly commendable, the power-oriented person's perfectionist needs translate achievements into humiliations. He no longer requires the neurotically competitive parent of yesteryear or the caustic critic to make the fruits of his labor turn to ashes; his inner values effect this translation automatically, and inwardly discourage future creative effort.

These are some of the snares of power which entrap creative fulfillment and vitiate life's energies. They make for many halfstarts toward creative achievement, and few full completions; this differential in time contributes to increasing self-doubt, self-contempt, and self-hatred, corroding the very sources and channels of self-realization.

The exaggerated sense of individual power is costly. It is bound to fail as a long term basis for emotional security, for where there is lacking a sense of faith in the feasibility of love and mutual constructiveness, then as Thomas Hobbes taught—in the context of political organization—there arises in man a "restless desire of power after power, that ceaseth only in death . . . because he cannot assure the power and means to live well, which he hath present, without the acquisition of more."

NOTES

[1] Many of the considerations—relative to this dichotomy of defenses—presented in this chapter were organized into a paper, "Implications of the Love-Power Value Differential," presented by me as part of a symposium on "Values in Group Psychotherapy," which took place early in 1958 at the Annual Conference of the American Group Psychotherapy Association.

V

POWER AND SELF-DEFEAT

This chapter is devoted to substantiating the paradoxical proposition that he who intensely craves the sense of individual power will often defeat himself so as to achieve this sense of power.

We start our discussion with the developmental basis for this pattern of self-defeat. It is this: The child soon learns that controlling the parent is a splendid way to achieve a sense of power. After all, the parent is obviously the most powerful being in the world: The parent controls everything of importance—good things to eat, dry clothes, interesting rattles, and so on. To be able to fetch this person "on the double," whenever one so much as whimpers, makes one a mighty puppeteer indeed, capable of manipulating others with verbal "strings." As we have seen, the sense of power binds anxiety; therefore the infant and child find power delicious and taste it in the context of omnipotence: If the cry can always bring the parent running, the young one feels all powerful within his microcosm, able with his voice to control the mightiest forces known to him.

It is normal to pass through this stage of sensed omnipotence. However, if the child's development is unfortunate, he may never outgrow the craving for unrealistic power. One possible meaning of stammering, for example, is that the listener is immobilized and must wait until the stammerer is good and ready to say what is forming on his lips; or, as Sullivan phrased it, the stammering serves to arrest "the flow of process in the world."

In time, the child learns that there are additional ways to control the parent: by balking, by *not* doing what the parent wants, by standing still when asked to walk, by running in a direction other than what the parent desires, and so on. Watch a child who has "his way," and see how intoxicating he finds having control over another. But the child soon learns that it is dangerous to oppose and control in a *direct* way. The parent spanks, and punishment hurts.

In healthful maturation the child therefore gives up excessively controlling the parent. But as we have already seen in detail, some infants and children cannot give up the power struggle. We have already noted the parental qualities that contribute to the retention and aggravation of this power struggle. Such a child faces this dilemma: People are unfriendly and must be combated, yet one must appear cooperative in order to get along. Direct expression of this excessive urge to power is therefore inhibited. But he learns that there is one way by which he can "have his cake" of controlling—and "eat it too." And that is by *defeating himself* at the same time as he controls the parent.

Were he to control and defeat his parents, though he succeeded, the activity would surely be hazardous, would surely bring swift punishment. But if he manipulates the parent while seeming to suffer and fail himself, the real issue would be clouded, and the power maneuver might well be effected quite safely. He thus learns at an early age that he can be excessively controlling, and yet avoid punishment—*if he uses a camouflage.* And the camouflage is this: Oppose your own interests while you oppose the will of your parent; appear to defeat yourself while you defeat your parent. The way to victory, for the child—to use the concept developed by Nietzsche, though the phrase is our own—is "self-and-other defeat."

Perhaps an illustration will make this point clearer. Let us suppose that Johnny, age four, has developed a power orientation, and defends himself from anxiety through controlling others. Let us also suppose that his parents plan a visit on a particular afternoon. Were Johnny to control and delay them in any direct way, he would soon feel their wrath. But if he vomits, has a fainting spell, or suffers some other "accident," the visit *is* held up, without direct punishment to him.

The controlling has thus been carried out, but at the cost of self-defeat for Johnny's comfort, or at the expense of regression to a less mature mode of behavior. Such controlling combines the will to power and a camouflage in the form of hurt to self—as in the old security operation of appearing to be less capable than one really is. Thus the child learns a "mechanism" that has fateful consequences for his self-realization. He learns that he can have a feeling of power—in a "safe" way—by defeating himself at the same time as he controls and defeats others.

This is seen in the child who is prone to somewhat camouflaged temper tantrums when the parent is exceedingly overbearing. To cooperate with such a parent is to lose one's individuality, to be permanently infantilized. On the other hand, to oppose the parent directly is hardly feasible from the child's position of utter dependence and weakness. However, in disguised tantrums, as in "involuntary" vomiting, reluctant learning, and protracted bed-wetting, reside relatively safe ways to oppose the parent, express one's own power, and bolster self-esteem through the sense of power. The self-defeat to the child's maturation and self-realization thus eventuating is, of course, obvious.

Consider the meaning of this, for it is important, yet perhaps difficult to grasp. In this mechanism of self-and-other defeat such a child has a ready opiate to lull present and future anxieties. This mechanism is always available to him. All he has to do is "turn it on." It is very easy to attain a sense of power through its use.

We go in a direction that is the result of many varieties of forces. When things are going our way, it is easy to be creative and constructive, to find a sense of emotional security and power through constructive effort. But when life is overwhelming, when we are blocked and frustrated time after time, when our anxieties emerge, and nightmares beset our sleeping hours, that is the time when we tend to fall back on less than mature ways of dealing with life. And at such times the more one has employed self-and-other defeat as a way of coping with anxiety, the more one will tend to use it again.

And so, in later years, such a person will tend to engage in similar self-defeat. In response to his anxieties, he will seek a sense of power through controlling others; and he will, for "safety's sake," habitually and without awareness of its full meaning, defeat himself at the same time. In the therapy situation, such a man will seek to control —by coming late, by asking unnecessary questions (with apparent intense earnestness), by being "unable" to recall essential material, and so on. Such persons experience quite severe anxiety when the therapist maintains his usual powers and prerogatives. They so inwardly fear and distrust people that they feel temporarily safe only when they are clearly in control. They will therefore seek repeatedly to control the therapist, to reproduce their pattern of binding anxiety through being powerful, through controlling. One young lady said in a moment of insight: "I used to ask questions of people, as I am tempted to do of you now, for no other reason than just to make them answer—to exercise my will."

There is now quite a substantial body of therapeutic literature on power's role in defeating therapy. One of the earliest pioneers, Karl Abraham, presented this point of view: The patient undermines and defeats his own attempts at psychotherapy because of the gnawing need to "keep the power of deciding" what he is going to give verbally during therapeutic sessions.

In a similar vein, Horney tells us that the need for absolute supremacy, for absolute power, sets the patient against his therapist: for the patient regards "any progress as a triumph for the analyst—a possible feather in the analyst's cap." The fact that the patient himself will benefit from such therapeutic progress is overridden by the urgent need for supremacy. The result is behavior which gives this sense of power, but destroys the analysis.

In the world outside the clinic, such people do analogous things: The student does not take the final examination, thereby upsetting the professor's plans, requiring a make-up examination, and incurring an automatic penalty in grade; the free-lance copywriter does not submit work on time, upsets the schedule of the agency, but also spoils vital career opportunities.

One gifted man never received his college diploma—because he would not submit one final book report for a course! And in the business career that followed, he "coasted along," earning far less, and doing far less, than he could. He simply *had* to have his way, and he defeated himself in the process.

In a life based largely upon the employ of the power mechanism those periods of time in which it breaks down are quite terrible to live through. In her efforts to keep her head and to avoid a "nervous breakdown" a certain woman sought treatment. Her life situation had changed recently, her husband refusing to put up any longer with the many power operations by which she had controlled him and the household for a score of years. "I don't know how I will be able to function," she said dejectedly, "if I am not completely in control of the situation."

This urgent need for a sense of power poses a severe threat to mental health, and may be so rigid and imperative that the individual may regress in order to restore such a sense of power.

In the instance noted, the woman had already resorted to hypochondriacal complaints, and continually called attention to her aches and pains as a way of tyrannizing her household. But should such hypochondria prove insufficient, she was inwardly prepared to regress further, quite possibly to pre-logical levels of personality organization, to insanity, in order to have "her way."

Power and self-defeat have been linked in philosophy. Friedrich Nietzsche's contributions represent a milestone in man's progress in this area of thought. Where his sense of being loved is deficient, Nietzsche taught, man desperately seeks the sense of power; and it is in the blind and heated quest for power that man effects his own destruction.

Nietzsche's own life clearly illustrates the coexistence of the two. His own conviction that the urge to personal power was basic in human personality ran not only through his *The Will to Power*, but was exemplified in his actual character, acted out as a principle for relating to his world; and the self-defeat which plagued his life ranged from the nihilism (to which he finally admitted), through the self-spoiling of opportunities for employment (until no one would permit him a teaching position), to the final catatonic outburst which heralded his terminal attack of insanity. [1]

The readiest source of the sense of personal power may be in passive "failure." The achievement of the sense of power through constructive activity may take months or even years of protracted effort; but by simply *not doing what is expected* of one, the sense of being a force to be reckoned with is readily obtainable in our world of social interdependence.

In appearing helpless may reside one's readiest potential for avoiding the demands made by others, and for rendering them ineffectual, for achieving what Horney terms "destructive domination." The executive who procrastinates in making necessary decisions, the spouse who simply cannot make up his mind on matters which vitally affect his mate, are through default controlling quite effectively and destructively.

The opiate of power exerts a subtle influence. Many of the inadequacies and shortcomings we ordinarily attribute to someone's being "shiftless" or "lazy" are in reality expressions of a driving and urgent hunger for power.

One executive, for example, let deadline projects pile up in his "in" basket although he knew there would be a day of reckoning when he would be called to account for not processing these important papers on time. As the days moved closer to the deadline, he would become progressively more anxious until, finally, full awareness of his procrastinating would break through his chronic "forgetting" and he—panic stricken—would begin to work on the project. He explained: "Something would come up—and I'd put it aside and say to myself—'I'll do it later.'" But "later" moved further and further away, until an inner alarm set off a flood of anxiety and sleepless nights. "I have the capacity to be on top of the job," he writhed, "and I *want* to do it. . . . And yet something holds me back!" The same "something," he discovered, caused him to thwart and disappoint his wife time and again. He would "forget" where they had arranged to meet; he would be "indecisive" about plans for vacation; he would be dense and insensitive about learning how to make love to her properly.

The same sort of basic emotional need was expressed in a homemaker who just could not get her housework done. "All I have to do is get up and move—and I'll get the housework finished," she would reproach herself repeatedly. "And yet, I sit and do nothing."

Both of them had to learn, before they could move ahead, that in doing "nothing" they were indeed doing a very important "something." And that was maintaining a sense of power by balking, by not doing what people expected them to do.

A similarly important self-defeating mechanism for maintaining a sense of power is to fail by one's own hand. This mechanism is a last resort for those who crave the sense of power, even as they sink in a sea of powerlessness. It is illustrated, in the extreme, by the man who defiantly kills himself in spite of the pleadings of onlookers. Even as he gives up his efforts to live and succeed in life, such a man can say to himself: "I *will die*. . . . It is *my* will to die!"

A parallel though less extreme sort of reasoning was revealed by a young man who habitually employed this mechanism, and who reported during a therapy session:

"That is the only thing I have under my power—to fail!"

Such power-hungry and despairing people are inwardly willing to undergo personal defeat providing that they have the power to decide the basis on which it will occur. Defeat—"*by my own hand*"—is not altogether defeat. It is a show of force for self-determination, an affirmation of will and power, which one can always marshal to bolster sagging self-esteem. As one man put it: "I am defeating myself in terms of one motive, but not in terms of another. . . . It is like a sacrifice play in baseball."

Self-defeat is therefore a technique for achieving a sense of power; for there *is* real power in partial or complete self-destruction: power to thwart and annoy the employer or teacher; power to disappoint or break the hearts of those who depend upon one's success; power to defy the fates and forces of the universe. In self-engineered failure or in suicide, one *is* master of one's fate.

"Whether I succeed or not is open to question," said the "sacrifice hitter" mentioned before. "I'm not accustomed to success. . . . But I *can* keep myself from kissing bottoms. . . . I have to avoid kissing bottoms—at *all* costs." It was presumably for this reason that he started four times to tell me a dream that session, and each time went off in another direction. Something else always seemed to come to mind, so that he never did get to complete the telling of the dream. "I don't like your prompting me," he growled, when I brought this meandering to his attention. And later, he saw clearly that he *never* wanted to complete the description of the dream: for in failing to complete it resided the power to keep me waiting, and in ignorance. Simply and truly he said, "I fail and I succeed at the same time."

Paradoxically, therefore, the power-oriented may affirm his power and will through failing and destroying his opportunities for self-realization in life. Defeat may thus be inwardly welcomed when it is *self*-defeat, when it is defeat "under my own power."

One aspect of such power resides in the forcing of punishment upon oneself. The psychiatrist Edmund Bergler described a similar concept under "psychic masochism" in his book *The Superego*: "It is not the bad mother (or her successive representatives) who is punishing me; *I*, through my initial provocation, made her punish me."

This constitutes one of the pitfalls self-defeatists create in therapy. They desperately need acceptance by another human being, yet often prod and provoke the therapist into disliking and rejecting them. And should they "succeed" here, they enjoy the flush of "victory"—though it is more truly defeat.

Theodor Reik has posited the theory that the masochist derives pleasure from his suffering, because such suffering is a prelude to eventual triumph over his adversary. The masochist maneuver follows the plan of losing a battle to insure the victory of a campaign. The "campaign" was begun long ago. The "war" itself may have been initiated by the inadequately loving parent who had so offended and undermined the child's self-esteem that less than best techniques for bolstering a drowning ego were desperately clung to. And one such technique was self-and-other defeat.

Deeply buried memories of early humiliations feed the fires of resentment. "You're going to make me feel helpless—no matter *what* I do!" protested a mature man during a therapy session. The resentment was real; its true target, however, was not I, but the parent. Yet I reaped the harvest sown by the parent; the patient continually transferred his parent's qualities to me, then perceived me as malevolent, and thus "defended" himself in our relationship. Such a man makes sure that no one will ever make him feel helpless again. For one thing, he goes his own way and tries never to "need" anyone any more.

As a child who had been badly hurt in relating to the parent, he later took pride in never asking the "tyrant" for anything. By extension, he *asked* nothing of life any more, but would only take and seize what he could, through craft. He would rather do without than request, or look openly to the kindness of others, rather seek to manipulate others into being forced to yield whatever he wanted. Whether it was a childish wish for a toy in years gone by, or an adult hunger for a sign of recognition, such a power-oriented individual would rather fail to obtain the material or symbolic thing desired, than achieve success through appealing to love and cooperation. He *prefers* to fail regarding these ordinary goals, providing he can succeed at achieving an inner understanding that he possesses the will power to refrain from making the request. In the extreme, this kind of psychology manifests itself in the waxy flexibility of catatonic schizophrenia, where the individual will not even permit pangs of hunger to cause him to ask for or to receive food, and may die if not tube fed.

Self-and-other defeat sometimes serves the purpose of achieving a belated mastery over a situation which had formerly been overwhelming. Where a parent or other authority figure had severely frightened the child and forced it to submit to coercion, the later child or adult may seek to defy authority, albeit through simultaneous self-defeat. By provoking oblique conflict with authority, the man can actively repeat a situation analogous to those which had been experienced more passively in childhood humiliations; the intense anxiety formerly felt in this parti-cular situation is not now fully re-experienced, and the in-dividual can undergo with some degree of pleasure the very situation which had once filled him with dread. There are instances of self-and-other defeat which warm the inner recesses of a heart which had long suffered humiliation, and under certain circumstances there is "glory" in them.

Where a quest for success has been chronically derogated by the destructive parent or supervisor, the child or adult may seek sustenance for self-esteem through self-engineered defeat. The parent or supervisor who continually changes plans on which the child's or subordinate's own plans must depend, may so burden him with memories of abortive efforts, as to crush attempts at future efforts.

Under these repeated "demonstrations" of his helplessness and powerlessness, the child or subordinate may no longer seek to create anything that really matters to him; a protective underestimation of one's creative urges and capabilities serves to avoid further humiliation. In such cessation of creative effort, there is at least self-determination and thin sustenance to self-esteem, however high the price to personal fulfillment; there is victory over the threat of total destruction to one's will and heart.

There occurs a subtle but devastating shift in such a person's orientation to the world of authority and supervisor-subordinate relationships. His approach is deflected from ways by which he may attain to self-realization to ways by which he may reap "victories" over the authority figure.

One such person came to see that his approach to the directives of authority figures could be expressed in terms of this childish formulation: "Is this something I *have* to do? Or, is it something I *ha-a-a-ve* to do?" The former was something he would make a point of ignoring, since he knew it to be a demand he could "get away" with; the latter was something he feared to ignore, and with which he would therefore grudgingly comply. The issue of advantage to self was not material, the point being simply whether or not the fear of immediate consequences, on the basis of the authority's power to enforce the directive, was sufficiently strong.

"It has become a fight," he reported, and his approach to life was not so much in terms of what it offered for self-realization as it was a quest for supporting his sense of personal power, through ignoring or otherwise thwarting authority and its intentions. This insight was verbalized only after considerable therapy; for the urge toward this fight had been deeply internalized, and had operated for years without conscious knowledge of motive. The "fight" had begun with parental attack upon the child's significance, either through actual neurotic competitiveness or a lack of sufficient affection and warmth; but the fight continues, and—barring therapeutic success—may be expected to continue for the remainder of the individual's life, long after the parent's overt influence has ceased to exist.

"Victory through defeat," Reik tells us, sums up the essence of masochism in modern man. To which we may add, that the "victories," although more apparent in early life over the tyrant-parent, in later years wax illusory, and the bitterness of self-defeat more real.

NOTES

[1] Nietzsche's theoretical contributions to the relationships between power and self-defeat are presented, with documentation, in *The Urge to Mass Destruction*, pages 158–167. An analysis of similar power elements in his personal life, and in the development of his mental illness, will be found in Chapter 5: "The Role of Mental Illness in the Creation of a Philosophy of Self-and-Other Defeat."

VI

SACRIFICES TO GUILT

According to an ancient Greek myth, Prometheus defied the cruel will of the ruling Power, stole fire from Zeus, and bestowed it, as an act of compassion, upon the human race. For this disobedience to the Father, for this presumption to self-will, the Titan suffered a tragic fall; he was chained to a rock and condemned to eternal torment.

This hero myth, as Otto Rank and others have developed at length, dramatizes the inner relations among the exercise of will, the influence of guilt, and the inner freedom for realizing the creative possibilities of selfhood.

This myth is especially applicable to our own time. For we have seen our culture, and the parents it tends to produce, as conducive to the generation of smoldering defiance within the child. And such inner resentment renders each of us particularly prone to the fate of Prometheus: to be chained—through our own guilt—to a level of existence which is beneath our creative potentials.

THE NATURE OF GUILT

Guilt is not easy to define. The very sensations involved in it are also difficult to describe clearly. Freud referred to a related "tension," and that is surely sensed. But we are usually thrown upon figurative devices, such as the expressions "pangs of conscience," "qualms of conscience," and "the heart is heavy," when we seek to convey what we feel when suffering guilt. It is similar to anxiety, since both serve as warning mechanisms and alert the individual to impending danger, but it differs in that it is a *specific form* of anxiety. While the relationships between anxiety and guilt are nebulous and controversial, yet we may say this much: that Freud conceived of guilt as a topical subdivision of anxiety. That is, anxiety refers to the general apprehension that something terrible may happen; whereas guilt occurs when the cause of this apprehension is specific —a sense of culpability, of having done wrong. More specifically: One is apprehensive lest one's own conscience withdraw its support.

To illustrate: If a person has the painful impression that something is going to happen, that he is shortly to be destroyed, this, so far, could be anxiety. But if investigation discloses the source to be a sense of culpability, of having transgressed against his conscience, then the feeling is properly termed guilt.

The "danger" in this specific form of anxiety—guilt— is that which is inside the individual himself: his own conscience. Where one fears punishment by some external agency, such as the police, for having committed some transgression, such feelings are not guilt, but rather fear. Guilt may properly be said to exist only when the danger is an internal one, when it is the conscience.

Let us note that there is a deeper danger than the conscience within ourselves. This danger is a primitive aggressiveness which Freud termed *Thanatos*, or the "death instinct." The conscience possesses power over us largely because its approval defends us against this more underlying threat. Understanding of the functional interrelationships between conscience and this underlying aggressiveness has been developed to some extent by Sigmund Freud, and later by Melanie Klein, Karl Menninger, and others. We note this deeper threat in passing, but will not attempt to discuss it definitively here, for it is too abstract and complex to permit brief discussion. Nevertheless, noting the existence of this factor, this primary aggressiveness or death instinct, permits an appreciation of various important qualities and influences of conscience which cannot be adequately explained without it. We shall mention some of these qualities and influences as we go along.

This all-important conscience is an inner "structure" within our personalities, and is a very real thing, largely the product of learning experiences. No one can comprehend the blocks to self-realization without understanding the nature and functions of conscience. This structure has long been known to exist. Saint Paul refers to it as a law written within men's hearts which functions to judge one's self. The term "conscience" was explicit in Roman moral writings of over twenty centuries ago. Modern thinkers, up through the present, have stressed its importance, in contexts ranging from Moral Sense liberalism through Kantian formalism and Freudian materialism.

The function of conscience is to *judge the self*. In the words of Freud, who termed this structure the "superego," its function consists of "observing and criticizing the self and exercising a censorship within the mind."

Although its function may often be unconscious, it is

nevertheless forceful and imperative. Immanuel Kant termed this function the "categorical imperative," and described its effect upon the man it condemns: "It follows him like a shadow, when he thinks to escape. He may indeed stupefy himself with pleasures and distractions, but cannot avoid now and then coming to himself or awakening, and then he at once perceives its awful voice. In his utmost depravity he may, indeed, pay no attention to it, but he cannot avoid *hearing* it." Indeed it does follow him. My own experience in psychotherapy is in agreement with the judgment of others—that guilt is generally more disturbing than is anxiety; and that it is considerably more difficult to help an individual dissolve the grounds of unrealistic guilt, than to do the same regarding anxiety.

The human *does* "hear" it; the "voice of conscience" becoming literally so in the awesome experiences of insanity. The deranged will often hear voices which criticize him, and which often refer to his sexual activities as dirty and despicable, and he often suffers from delusions of being "watched," a phenomenon which Freud and others have taken to be a direct reference to the self-observation of the conscience.

The conscience may be conceived to consist of two parts, which differ in their genealogy and function. Erich Fromm has termed these the "humanistic conscience" and the "authoritarian conscience." We shall see important considerations which stem from this difference.

The authoritarian conscience derives from experiences with one's parent. Its injunctions are related to introjections of demands made by the parent. These parental demands were originally the most important criteria of "good" and "bad" for the child; observance of them would bring in its train parental acceptance and therefore a sense of personal goodness; whereas disobedience became associated with being rejected and therefore with feelings of worth-lessness. In time, the mother is internalized through intro-jection. That is, these parental injunctions are initially out-side the child, but soon come to exist within the child's own personality—a phenomenon readily explicable in terms of the usual laws of learning.

Once this internalization has occurred, a conscience prop-erly exists within the personality. Just as the parent influenced the child by granting proofs of affection or by threats of withdrawing her affection, so does the con-science come to operate: by giving support to one's sense of goodness, or by undermining it. As long as the thing which is feared is outside oneself, as is the parent, the related feeling is no more than a social fear or anxiety. But after the conscience has come to operate and is feared, we have true *guilt*.

Thus, we have a most significant transition from an *external* disciplining agent to an *internal* one. It is no longer an external danger which is feared, but an inner representative of this danger. This conscience takes the place of the parental function and thereafter observes, admonishes, and threatens the self, in the same way as the parents formerly did the child. It is now a fairly independent "watchman" who gives the alarm when some-thing approaches which formerly might have resulted in the loss of the mother's affection. It now operates as an "inner mother," as the psychoanalyst Otto Fenichel terms it.

The mother had nurtured one's self-esteem by bestowing love and other things. Now, the conscience takes on a similar role: Complying with it brings feelings of worth and emotional security; violating its injunctions brings feel-ings of guilt, similar to those experienced by the child when he believes he is rejected by the parent. And this feeling is the one the conscientious person aims to avoid.

So, the conscience takes over the regulation of self-esteem. The direct fear of consequences, of course, still continues to operate; but much of the regulating role of approval or rejection by externalities is now taken over by the inner understanding that one has done or not done the "right" thing.

Mild guilt feelings, as mild anxiety, serve as warnings that far more severe feelings, possibly overwhelming feelings, are on their way, and that steps should be initiated to forestall their appearance. These intense guilt feelings attend a terrible loss of self-esteem and emotional security, the extreme being feelings of annihilation, as occur in severe depression.

Unfortunately, this authoritarian conscience, being largely in the "form" of the significant parent, may be as unhealthy and unloving as was that parent. And where this inner representative of outer reality is sick, it may actually give its approval to the self when it behaves self-destructively; conversely, it may severely threaten the self when it behaves constructively regarding the unfolding of its potentials.

A young woman, with a conscience of this sort, was relatively at peace with life while she wasted years in unfortunate liaisons; she became severely guilt-ridden when she sought to make a good and lasting relationship with a man. In the latter instance, she was being a "traitor" regarding the values taught by her mother and incorporated within her conscience. The self behaves toward the conscience much in the way it once behaved toward a potentially threatening parent whose acceptance and forgiveness it needed.

Patients in therapy often relate to the therapist in the same way they do to their own consciences. One repeatedly opened each session with "How are you today?" and then would remain silent, expecting me to tell her. It surprised and shocked her that most patients launch immediately into talking about *themselves:* "I have a feeling," she said, "that the things I feel are inconsequential. . . . I feel so *guilty* when I talk about myself!" Why did she feel so guilty about paying attention to her own needs and feelings? She later associated, when in a depressed mood: "Children were the source of my mother's troubles—her lingering illness. . . . Or so she would tell me. I guess I *always* had the feeling that I was 'bad'—that I made 'trouble.' "

Barring psychotherapeutic intervention, the conscience is not prone to change, but rather tends to maintain its original form through all the years of life. While Freud had originally believed that the superego was not in substantial operation until about the fifth year of life, there is evidence—as shown in the work of Melanie Klein—that it is in full operation slightly before the third year.

Since the child's understanding during this early period is primitive, and may be unrealistic, a hostile parent may leave an impression of *extreme* viciousness and hostility not actually possessed. And the introjected conception—the conscience—may therefore functionally manifest these vicious qualities, which the parent was "believed" to truly possess.

Thus it was that this self-disparaging woman's conscience, largely in the "form" of the mother she remembered from early childhood, continued to blame her. She had, within herself, a "voice" which harshly admonished her to be more and more interested in others, and to turn from consideration of herself.

Still another factor making for harshness and even viciousness in one's conscience is this: There is evidence, albeit clinical and inferential, that one's original aggressive impulses—the "death instinct"—are somehow "employed" by the conscience, so that its cruelty may be far in excess of any example posed by the parent's actual behavior. We are led to this conclusion by the following sorts of occurrences: People who are clearly at odds with their consciences often display a fury toward the self (in, for example, an implacable bent to annihilate oneself) that exceeds by far the ambivalence study reveals the parent to have possessed toward the developing child. Where did this "extra" vindictiveness come from? The best theory to date is that this additional severity emanates from the "death instinct," which somehow is released from within and surges out toward the self when the "protection" of conscience is withdrawn. It is in clinical depression, in melancholia, that the workings of such a conscience are most salient and readily studied. It is here that the utter cruelty of the conscience is most discernible: its hatred of the self and of its very life.

As one becomes a more sophisticated observer, the self-destructive role of conscience in less extreme maladjustment also comes into view. "I hate myself!" voiced in a therapeutic interview by a self-defeating young woman, may be an attitude harbored by far more people than we commonly suppose.

Thus, our authoritarian conscience may be monstrously unwise or cruel, and it may encourage or discourage our doing things regardless of whether these things are intrinsically good or bad, of whether or not they assist self-realization. But in contrast, the humanistic portion of the conscience transcends the attributes of any particular authority figure; its sympathies are rather rooted in the best interests of the living. It respects life, and appears to hold happiness and self-realization as its criteria of goodness. While admittedly vague, we shall nevertheless find these statements to have important (if ill-defined) meaning for the processes which govern the evolution of selfhood.

As to terminology, when we henceforth employ the term "conscience" we shall generally mean the authoritarian portion—the functional entity Freud had in mind when he termed it the "superego." On the other hand, when reference is made to the humanistic portion of the conscience *alone*, which will be seldom, it will be so stated. We shall also distinguish between the terms "guilt" and "guilt feeling." The former is a *condition* which exists when the conscience condemns the self; the latter is a feeling state which may or may not accompany that condition. In brief, guilt exists when the conscience finds the self has fallen short of its standards, and therefore withdraws its support of self-esteem; but guilt feeling can coexist with guilt only when the individual's system of psychological defenses permits such feelings to emerge into awareness. If, for example, repression is much used, then the individual may possess guilt without experiencing any guilt feeling.

This distinction between the two is an important one. Much of the harm which befalls self-realization (on the basis of guilt) does so because the human harbors guilt, but seeks to avoid painful guilt feelings; and his devices for avoiding such feelings often extensively curtail his inner freedom for fulfilling the constructive possibilities of his life. We shall generally employ the term *guilt* to denote both "guilt" and "guilt feeling," but shall take care to employ the terms precisely when such distinction is essential to our discussion.

GUILT AND SELF-REALIZATION

We have seen how certain experiences during development years can produce deep and largely unconscious resentment within the growing individual; and that this resentment is often accompanied by an intense wish for revenge, as well as by tendencies toward the provocation and perpetuation of frictions and difficulties with authority figures.

One's own authoritarian conscience, cast largely in the form of the insufficiently loving parent, is hardly likely to be permissive toward the harboring of such hostility. It is rather more likely to be as harsh, rejecting, and inexorable as was the parent prototype. Moreover, while the child or adult can often disguise his hostility toward the authority figure through passive-aggressive and similar techniques, these camouflages fail to shield him from his own conscience. The outer authority figure may only perceive "illness" or "inability" to function; but the inner conscience senses the true, albeit largely unconscious motive, and condemns the self for the underlying hostility.

Therefore, a consequence of being insufficiently loved in childhood, as mediated by the developing unconscious hostility and the developing modes of reaction to this hostility, is often a permanent and sizable fund of guilt which may cripple the creative capacities during the course of one's entire life. For where there is guilt there is a need to suffer, and once the inner sense of guilt is loose in the personality, there is need to experience punishment in *some* form, and some of these forms of punishment are severely injurious to self-realization.

How do we know there is guilt when the person is not

aware of guilt feelings? Freud wrestled with this question, as he observed: "Patients do not easily believe what we tell them about an unconscious sense of guilt. They know well enough by what torments (pangs of conscience) a conscious feeling of guilt, the consciousness of guilt, can express itself, and so they cannot admit that they could harbor entirely analogous feelings in themselves without observing a trace of them." He offered the following solution: "I think we may meet their objection by abandoning the term 'unconscious feeling of guilt,' which is in any case an incorrect one psychologically, and substitute for it a 'need for punishment' which describes the state of things observed just as aptly. We cannot, however, let ourselves be prevented from judging and localizing this unconscious feeling of guilt in the same way as we do the conscious variety."

In brief, we infer the existence of guilt because the person manifests in his behavior a tendency toward experiencing suffering, a need for punishment; and this inference appears sound, in spite of a complete absence of attendant *feelings* of guilt.

In therapy, it is quite a difficult task to help people become *aware* of their need to suffer, even though these very people give ample evidence of such a need. You may repeatedly call attention to their smiling when telling of personal misfortunes; you may point time and again to specific ways by which they take unnecessary risks in life; and yet they cling stubbornly to a functional "blindness" in the matter.

Freud saw this need to suffer as the basic reason why some people did not progress in therapy. He said: "In the end we come to see that we are dealing with what may be called a 'moral' factor, a sense of guilt, which is finding atonement in the illness and is refusing to give up the penalty of suffering."

Yet we are often successful in helping people become aware of this need to suffer. One such person clearly had mixed feelings about this "success," reporting with no little resentment: "Well, today I *felt* the need to suffer if *that's* any accomplishment!" But her mood changed, some sessions later, as she sensed a forward breakthrough: "I feel *such* guilt," she said. "If I could only confess and get some kind of open punishment I would be relieved."

This need for punishment is related to the need for inner peace. The child had learned that atoning for one's transgression—through suffering the punishment inflicted by the parent—had brought in its wake a period of reconciliation, forgiveness, and peace. Analogously, in his life with the "inner parent"—the superego—inwardly aware of his largely unconscious hostility toward authority, he also seeks forgiveness from this superego; and the payment for absolution is personal suffering. The pain and suffering are accepted so as to lessen pressure from the conscience, to regain the self-esteem lost consequent to rejection by the conscience, and to be reassured against possible feelings of annihilation.

Where the parent had been stern and unrelenting, the child may have gathered the impression that punishment was quite sure to be meted out and that even though indefinitely delayed, there was no chance of its being overlooked or forgotten. The eventuating adult, in analogous relations with his conscience, will tend to feel unrelenting guilt over his transgressions—guilt which will remain unrelieved until atonement in some form has been effected. Thus, the eventuality of punishment in childhood adds to this adult wish to "pay" and "get it over with."

Strange as it may seem, there is an *amount* of suffering —a "quota of suffering"—each must meet. As Freud put it, there is a "certain level of suffering" which must be maintained in each of our lives. The amount of suffering required to meet this "quota" varies greatly from individual to individual. Its size depends upon the degree to which each is condemned by his own conscience. If this quota is not met, then guilt tends to break into awareness in the form of guilt feelings which may well prove unbearable. Severe guilt feelings carry a connotation of doom and impending disintegration. It is to avoid these that one hastily seeks to meet one's quota of suffering, to experience pain less agonizing than the expectation of imminent annihilation. This concept of *amount* of suffering as compensation for some transgression has long been acknowledged. It is implicit in the principle of talion, according to which a crime may be "undone" by the infliction of similar suffering upon the original transgressor. Talion is the basis of widespread rituals of penitence and atonement.

Phenomena of *transition of symptoms* repeatedly attest to the validity of the statement that a quantum of suffering is required at any time. Freud has repeatedly pointed to the fact that when one form of suffering is alleviated, another form of suffering frequently takes its place, and that as long as guilt remains severe, the loss of one neurotic symptom will only mean its prompt replacement by another. Examples of this are numerous. When the weather became milder and a man's arthritic pains were eased, his insomnia and feelings of depression markedly increased. Conversely, when a young lady underwent serious surgery, her severe phobic symptoms and free-floating anxiety practically disappeared for the entire period of convalescence, but reappeared as soon as she was well.

Freud offers examples, then summarizes: "It is instructive, too, to find, against all theory and expectation, that a neurosis which has defied every therapeutic effort may vanish when the person has become involved in the misery of an unhappy marriage, has lost his fortune, or has developed a dangerous organic disease. The one form of suffering has then given way to another, and all that mattered, as we see, was that a certain level of suffering should be maintained."

Caught between the pressures of various impulses and the demands of conscience, as between the desire for sexual release and internalized parental injunctions, a person may not be able to completely desist from acting out these inner demands for impulse gratification. He may, however, bribe the superego with "gifts" of personal suffering. If one suffers enough, then the superego may be pacified and one may repeat the process, may again express the forbidden impulse, once more atone. This may be repeated indefinitely as the manifestation of a quality termed by the psychoanalyst Franz Alexander, the "corruptibility of the superego."

Some compulsive acts represent, in part, ways of meeting the quota of suffering. A personal ritualistic ceremony, such as the compulsive checking of gas jets, often represents a protective measure against forbidden impulses—a prevention or undoing of some imaginary aggressive action. In addition, such prolonged checking, often compulsively engaged in at the very time when the individual is late for an appointment, carries a sizable quantity of personal embarrassment and suffering. It is, in brief, what Freud terms a "self-punitive symptom."

Some cyclical symptoms, that is, the alternation of two varieties of symptom, may be explained in terms of the concept of the corruptibility of the superego. If an instinctual urge finds expression in one variety of neurotic symptom (such as neurotic sexual behavior), the payment to conscience may be made through another, self-punitive variety of symptom (as compulsive self-humiliation); and when the conscience has thus been bribed, the cycle may be repeated, making the individual's life largely an alternation of neurotic instinctual expression and punitive symptoms.

When the demands of the conscience are so severe that they cannot be met, depression may result. Melancholia means that the conscience has not been satisfied, has refused to forgive, has withdrawn its support of self-esteem, and has permitted underlying aggressiveness to be directed against the self. In the extreme, suicide occurs: The aggressiveness directed against the self often kills that self.

Superegos vary considerably in severity. The individual with a superego fashioned after a loving and permissive parent will generally have a relatively small quota of suffering to meet, whereas the one with a harsh and adamant superego will be weighed down in life by a large quota even when his life behavior is relatively innocent. Few efforts are so doomed to failure as those which seek to ingratiate the self with a superego which is intrinsically harsh, unloving, implacable, and unforgiving. For it will demand the impossible: that one serve others to fantastic degrees; that one cause all members of one's family, for example, to be happy, healthy, and successful. If one member be unhappy, ill, or in trouble, such a conscience will storm disapproval, causing continual feelings of unworthiness and guilt.

There exist various non-creative patterns for meeting one's world—character patterns which directly contribute toward meeting one's quota of suffering, but which do not advance the emergence of constructive selfhood. We have seen this quota, and its concomitant size, to follow from one's burden of guilt; and the guilt, in turn, to follow from the condemnation of self by one's own conscience. Self-destructive characterological tendencies and non-creative modes of behaving in the social group may serve to meet the quota of suffering, and to prevent the actual guilt feeling.

Chronic alcoholism is one such pattern. The alcoholic repeatedly exposes himself to the scorn of his peers and punishes his self-concept as severely as his physical constitution. Passivity in the face of abuse is another. In our time, women often absorb an enormous amount of abuse from their husbands over a period of many years. The innate intelligence and forcefulness of such women frequently stand in marked contrast to the obsequious role in which they have been cast in marriage; guilt over one thing or another is often a major cause. Separating herself from another—from her parent, or perhaps psychologically from her husband, differentiating herself and achieving status as an individual—is often one of the roots of such guilt. Getting oneself abused is still another. It may parade under the guise of overconscientiousness, concern for one's family, or involvement with friends. But when the day comes that one finally recognizes the pattern and asks "Why do I get pushed around so easily?" the answer is often traced to a need for abuse and punishment.

Marriage is an especially fertile field for reaping one's quota of suffering. A poor choice of partner guarantees a lifetime harvest. Freud observed that "unhappy marriage" and "bodily infirmity" are the two things which most often "dissolve" a neurosis: "They both gratify especially the sense of guilt (need for punishment) which binds many neurotics so fast to their neuroses. By a foolish choice in marriage they punish themselves; a long organic illness they regard as a punishment by fate and then often cease to keep up their neurosis."

Self-mutilation is yet another means of meeting the quota. Unconsciously hostile people often bite their finger-nails to the quick, and tend to bite more persistently when the hostility is particularly provoked. A young patient recalled that she would mark and mutilate library books while reading, and she would also alternately rip the skin of her hand. This duality may be thus illustrated: Unconscious hostility, ill-directed outward, required its quota of unconscious hostility (guilt) ill-directed inward.

The giving up of ordinary human satisfactions (asceticism) may be so employed. Going without, hungering, may be used for softening the fury of a conscience, much as the "hunger strike" is used to protest the sentence of a severe judge in a court of law. Two areas of human satisfaction often sacrificed for this purpose are those of sex and food. It little avails to thrust proper opportunities for the enjoyment of either of these upon such an ascetic, so long as his quota of suffering is gapingly unfilled, and so long as his guilt is overwhelming. Where satisfactions are thrust upon such an individual, various devices come to his aid, so as to forestall a deluge of guilt feeling. The woman, for example, whose sexual abstinence has served to meet her quota of suffering and self-hurt will not become sexually well adjusted simply because time passes in her marriage; instead we may expect her to remain frigid, or to find normal sex relations actually painful. Moreover, opportunities for normal sex relations posed by her marriage may threaten to upset her inner economy, her established ways of meeting her quota; so that these very normal opportunities may precipitate severe anxiety and guilt.

The holiday season poses threats to such an unconsciously ascetic individual. One conscientious secretary reported plaintively that she had been receiving Christmas gifts all week long, in far greater abundance than she had expected, and that the symptoms for which she had come under treatment were worsening with each new unexpected gift.

One mechanism employed for meeting such unexpected and inwardly unwanted good fortune is to deny "enjoying" it. An unconsciously hostile young man, who labored under a markedly harsh conscience, reported on the beauty of the oceanside where he had spent his weekend. It was a glowing account of the loveliness of the place. When he finished, he added a quick epilogue: "But I didn't *enjoy* it!" The same was true of the company of the ladies he knew, his minor triumphs at work, and every ordinary area of satisfaction. The hazard to inner economy implicit in "enjoyment" was more than he could tolerate. For some guilt-ridden people there is an alternation between suffering and the ability to enjoy. "I notice that on the days when I suffer a lot," one reported, "then, after the hours of suffering—I can go out and enjoy myself. . . . I can then see a movie and laugh my head off." Others can find pleasure only under circumstances in which they play "Russian roulette." One such university professor found in extramarital affairs which jeopardized his career enjoyment of a degree that his extremely attractive wife could never provide.

"Prosperity" is difficult for these people to bear. An artist who finally managed to arrange for a six month period in which she could devote herself entirely to painting reported: "I now have nightmares every night. . . . I wake up screaming. I say to myself—'You've got too much. . . . You're not suffering enough.'"

Such people may delight in their own misfortune. They

seek an "accident." The professor mentioned saw the road to be under construction on his way to work, and he sensed "glee." "In a way," he reported, "I'd *like* to have an accident."

Further physical illness may contribute toward meeting the quota. It is a common observation of clinicians that various physical symptoms, such as indigestion, often markedly worsen when some good fortune is met, and lessen conversely when life is objectively more difficult. Various rites involving symbolic self-mutilation apparently also serve this purpose; too, specific symptoms which cause unusual distress may fill this function. One guilt-ridden individual, for example, would often sense a darkening of his visual field, and would fear he was losing his sight. This man happened to be markedly visually oriented, obtaining much pleasure through what he saw. The fear of going blind, for him, represented severe suffering. It hardly appears coincidental that such visual symptoms occurred shortly after he had seen or thought something which aroused sexual or hostile thoughts or feelings which provoked guilt.

Let us summarize our discussion. We have seen that the operations of conscience—the effects of guilt—may cause severe inroads upon our freedom for self-realization. The pangs of conscience are highly useful as a "warning signal" to be heeded by the self, by the ego; but these very signals of conscience can be highly injurious to self when their influence extends beyond this warning function. When the conscience functions in too rigid or automatic a manner, when its influence is too far separated from reality, its signals may cause an overreaction by the individual. Its role may decrease as a signaler of danger, and it may, rather, become overly important in itself, i.e., defense against guilt feelings may become the all-consuming task of the individual's life. Such a defensive orientation may play havoc with creative potential. For the conscience punishes for acts *contemplated*, for thoughts, as well as for deeds. In the unconscious, the wish to do the forbidden is similar to the actual carrying out of the wish as far as condemnation by the conscience is concerned. Therefore, the covert life, the thinking and feeling life, may become inhibited and constructed so as to avoid giving offense to the conscience, thus leading inexorably to the impoverishment of creative inner processes. The conscience operates vigorously, even though it is largely unconscious. That its condemnation—that guilt—is often unconscious does not in the least render it the less influential, but rather increases its hazard to self-realization; for such unconscious guilt makes for free-floating guilt feelings, which must be kept in abeyance. The mechanisms of defense against these guilt feelings may be unquestionably undermining to the realization of creative potentials.

Of the sources of guilt, perhaps the one which is deadliest stems from failure to be what one deeply *wants* to be. This inner conception of what one wants to be is related to parental teachings, but may also be very different in its genealogy. For this portion of the conscience, sometimes termed the "ego-ideal," embraces precepts and examples which are in addition to those supplied by the family. It is similar, but not identical, to what Erich Fromm terms the "humanistic conscience." It condemns each of us severely for not making the most of creative potentials; and if one is excessively servile to the whims of unwise authority, and yields too readily the birthright of creative self-determination, then, warns Otto Rank, we feel ourselves guilty on account of the "unused life," the "unlived" in us. This hatred of the self for wasting its opportunities for life is a more important human dynamic than is generally supposed. It emerges more clearly at the climacteric, and is believed to be a major cause of that serious mental illness often seen at this time of life—involutional melancholia. For there is a day of reckoning when each asks himself what he had done with his life. And where too much of the self's possibilities have been sacrificed to appease the authoritarian conscience, the hatred for self may exceed human tolerance and undermine the very will to live.

Therefore, the guilt-ridden individual welcomes the heavy hand of fate, the misfortune he can clearly attribute to the actions of others, and he finds that suffering "best" which gives least cause for healthy segments of his conscience to accuse him of that which he is *truly* guilty, namely, some form of self-defeat. In this context, it is understandable that the self-defeatist inwardly welcomes humbling misfortune. Caught between a harsh superego which demands its quota of suffering, and "humanistic" elements of conscience which despise self-defeat, few things bring such immediate emotional safety as "stubbing one's toe" on the experiences of life.

The particular form of suffering is not important, Freud tells us; it is rather the suffering and self-hurt itself that matters. And therefore the "moral masochist," he teaches, the one who labors under a severe burden of guilt, "always holds out his cheek whenever he sees a chance of receiving a blow."

VII

FURTHER INFLUENCES OF GUILT

We have noted that many people are not free to succeed. If events beyond their control should thrust good fortune upon them they become one of those whom Freud has termed "wrecked by success."

In this chapter, we shall continue to explore the role of guilt in such self-induced "wrecking," and pay particular attention to guilt's influence upon the ability to succeed, the inner freedom to "follow through" constructively to actual achievement.

We have developed the concept of the "quota of suffering," and seen that if this quota is unfilled the guilt-laden individual will surely find ways to fill it.

One such way is to suffer *part* destruction. Here the formula for self-preservation is that if one suffers injury to a part of oneself, he may propitiate the avenging forces of the conscience, and save the "whole" from being destroyed. It is as if, through pleading guilty to a minor charge—through accepting a lesser evil—one pays a small price to avert an overwhelmingly huge, dreaded destructive force. It is the psychology of sacrifice in ritual: The scapegoat, a small part of one's property or self, is offered to atone for the past, and to protect the future. In Freudian terms, a part is offered for the whole; tribute in suffering is offered in order to avoid the more complete disaster of "castration."

Self-defeat is one variety of such token destruction. It is a "lesser evil," a substitution of part destruction so as to avoid a complete annihilation of self. In its more passive form, such self-defeat consists in ignoring, or in using but minimally, one's capacities and capabilities for dealing with life. Characteristically, such self-defeatists experience relative inner peace when their native talents are idle, and will come down with severe guilt and depression when attempting to work constructively.

In more active forms of self-defeat, there is "prophylactic autocastration," to use the term employed by the psychoanalyst Otto Fenichel. There is an active undercutting of one's own power for succeeding, so as to prevent possible retaliation by competitive and hostile forces such as those associated with one's own conscience. In one such instance, a young woman felt impelled to tell even passing strangers some of the more embarrassing features of her life. She craved self-esteem, but so inwardly feared retribution by a tyrannical conscience that she continually took active measures to undercut her actual status in the eyes of all, including her own.

This sort of activity represents what Freud has termed "moral masochism." It is distinguished from sexual or "erotogenic" masochism and involves self-inflicted suffering as the result of a need for punishment.

A dramatic form taken by this need for punishment is described by Freud as "the criminal from a sense of guilt." It was a surprise, Freud relates, to discover that in many criminals a powerful but largely unconscious sense of guilt existed *before* the crime, and was therefore a cause of criminal behavior rather than a result. The crime sometimes serves the purpose of giving the guilt something to which to attach itself. The commission of such a crime affords relief from guilt, on the basis of permitting this unconscious sense of guilt to fasten onto something real and immediate, and through the punishment likely to ensue. Children, too, Freud continues, are often naughty "on purpose" so as to provoke punishment, and are quiet and relatively contented after chastisement, a phenomenon also related to guilt. By provoking the outer world of parents or substitutes to inflict external punishment upon them, the child and adult save themselves from some of the severity of internal self-punishment.

In this light we can see why a child did the following "unreasonable" thing: She would first steal all the change out of her mother's purse, and then insist that her mother look into that same purse for a coin to give her. In this way she insured that her stealing would be noticed, and that she would be punished; for the pressure of guilt— over other "transgressions"—was more than she could bear.

When punishment serves essentially to placate guilt, it fails as a disciplinary device. This is part of the tragedy implied in a penal system which metes out punishment without comprehending the psychological structure of the particular criminal. The unconscious sense of guilt may inexorably drive the recidivist to further violation of the law, and to further imprisonment, which brings relief from such guilt however much it defeats self-realization. A self-defeating individual whose activities fall short of crime may avoid prison, yet effectively destroy his opportunities for personal fruition through a similar need, satisfied through similar self-provoked punishments and penalties imposed by others.

Weekends and holidays tend to upset the suffering

status, since they pose relief from workday trials. Characteristically, guilt-ridden individuals' symptoms of suffering worsen when faced with a weekend of leisure, or when a holiday is in the offing. For such persons, "success" may precipitate tremendous anxiety and guilt. A minor success brings a relapse of symptomatology; a windfall is precursor to panic. For that matter, any good fortune may upset the balance, and plunge the individual into excruciating anxiety and feelings of guilt; an instance comes to mind of the salesman who encountered a windfall in the form of an unusually large commission and who immediately suffered severe anxiety and guilt, together with a worsening of other symptoms.

Apparently, as long as the quota of suffering remains constant, an improvement in one area of a man's life must be counterbalanced by increased suffering in some other area. Similarly, a man with large holdings in securities reported: "I feel more uneasy when the stock market goes up than when it goes down." Such a person becomes frightened or guilt laden when he improves under treatment. A man in this position reported, "For the first time in my life I have no complaints about my life, my work, my boss, my supervisor. . . . And it *frightens* me!"

This is why such people fear success in psychotherapy. One young woman who had suffered intense and prolonged anguish at the hands of her husband, gradually learned how to avoid being hurt by him. Then she reported: "Now that I have become less vulnerable to his attacks, now that he does not hurt me as much I feel *guilty* for not being hurt by his attacks. . . . I feel that I *have* to be punished; and if he is not punishing me, then I must punish myself—with guilt!"

This crippling of one's own power to achieve success is dramatically illustrated by the "negative therapeutic reaction" we have noted earlier, the failure of the patient in psychotherapy to move ahead at a time when he appears quite ready for such progress. For such patients, Freud wrote that there is a "force" at work which is defending the self against recovery, and is clinging tenaciously to illness and suffering. "We have recognized that part of this force is the sense of guilt. . . ." This "moral factor," this need to atone, this largely unconscious sense of guilt, posed "the most difficult resistances and the greatest menace to the success of our medical or educative aims." And other psychoanalysts agreed with Freud that one of the most difficult tasks in psychotherapy is that of conquering a severe, unconscious sense of guilt.

As to the developmental aspect of this subject the essence resides in how "well" the parent loved the child. Specifically, it resides in how well the parent resolved her own competitiveness, and how free she had been to let the child develop his own powers and capabilities. Where the parent is hostile toward the child's maturation of powers and potentials, problems are bound to arise which curtail the child's freedom to succeed; some parents go to bizarre lengths to crush the child's will and prolong its dependence upon them. That a parent will compete with her own child for power and status is an understanding we are loath to accept. But clinicians are accustomed to seeing the results of such neurotic competitiveness in the underachieving children and adults who are thus produced. "Everything I try to learn or do, my mother tries to take away from me!" is the sort of complaint heard from the underachieving person when he becomes sufficiently free to perceive what is taking place in his life.

Such antagonism toward the child's developing will and powers is by no means limited to the mother. Fathers, siblings, relatives—all may single out a child and oppose its will to fantastic extents. And a strange element is this: For some reason, one particular child in a household is often singled out to be dominated; and the others in the household—even younger children—intimidate this child, and remind him continually of his alleged intrinsic inferiority. A result of such domination is the gradual building up within the child of a tremendous hostility which is relegated to the unconscious out of fear of reprisal. This hostility is largely oriented toward the parent, the figure of authority; and since the child's conscience is fashioned after the parent, it condemns him because of this largely unconscious resentment. The result is not only an overly dominated child, but also a guilt-ridden child. Just as the parent opposed the growth of power and capability in the child, so does part of the conscience, for it is modeled after this parent. Therefore, when the person seeks to behave creatively or discovers some new power in himself he is condemned by his tyrant superego, and suffers pangs of guilt. He comes inwardly to perceive the exercise of his own will and creative intelligence as being a rebellion against authority's prerogatives. One pathetically blocked and unproductive individual reported, as he made contact with his underlying feelings: "Every time I try to do anything for myself—arrange for anything—I feel so terribly guilty!"

Such a person will tend to feel unworthy of success. He cannot expect "fate" to grant anything so good. "I'm not worthy of such happiness, I don't deserve it," is Freud's formulation of the phenomenon; and he continued: "But these two motives are essentially the same, for one is only a projection of the other. For, as has long been known, the fate which we expect to treat us so badly is a materialization of our conscience, of the severe superego within us, itself a residue of the punitive agency of our childhood."

Such an individual's dreams often reveal severe condemnation by an authority figure (conscience) over harboring the urge to realize the full limits of his capabilities. He may manifest the conflicting need to avoid such fruition. For one man, this assumed the form of recoil from achieving a professional level higher than that which his self-defeating brother had reached (it being pertinent that this brother had been the "man of the house" after his father's early death). For an attractive young lady, the conflict was known in the following form: "I have usually made a 'zero' person out of myself—and then people accepted me; but when I showed my brains or beauty, they rejected me. So now, I always leave something out when I prepare for a party—so that if girls are there, they won't dislike me." Actually, the conflict was not so much between the young lady and her peers as it was between herself and her own conscience. Thus, she would disparage herself before others for a defensive purpose, but her problem essentially involved the making of an adjustment to her own conscience, rather than adjusting to others.

Another young woman with a similarly overbearing conscience, whose mother had sought for years to make her fantastically dependent and ineffectual, finally obtained suitable employment for herself; her associations on that event were "Cheating! Cheating!" which we can readily understand in relation to her conscience's reaction to these efforts at self-differentiation and self-determination.

Such people tend to feel terribly guilty over any "success" in the exercise of will function. Success in some competition, in thinking critically, in looking after one's business or job, or even in selecting advantageous elective courses at school tends to unleash anxiety and guilt. For such will function represents, in some measure, rebellion against authority; and the intensity of guilt follows in part from the urge to displace the unloving parent, to be a *better* parent than the actual one has been.

"Why is it that I can't have *conviction* in my sales approach?" a man with this sort of problem asked. For he had observed a fellow salesman in action, and was struck by the apparent "sincerity" the other man displayed, which contrasted sharply with his own manner. And the answer his analysis came up with repeatedly was this: His own inner judge, his conscience, did not give wholehearted support to his efforts; and this inner "house divided" showed up as an apparent lack of "integrity" and "sincerity." Since his sense of personal significance is not well buttressed by early experiences—in psychoanalytic terms, his "narcissistic supplies" are deficient—such an individual remains dependent upon the parent's approval. In the event that this approval is not forthcoming, he is immediately inundated by anxiety and guilt; his self-esteem falters without continual support of this sort. His anticipation of impending punishment is a gross exaggeration of the threats actually posed by reality. An inwardly blocked young man associated: "When I try to work—to do something I like to do—I sense the feeling that something *terrible* is going to happen. . . . What might happen?" he asked rhetorically, and continued: "My father might kill me. . . . When I was a child my father would chase me and threaten me. . . . He was against everything I wanted. . . . It was terrible!"

Since the guilt-laden individual has inner feelings of unworthiness, he tends to be assailed from within by feelings of ineptitude if he happens to find himself in a position of leadership. He therefore is overly dependent upon "support" from others. A college instructor with such feelings recalled how very much he needed his wife's phone call the night of his first lecture: "I *needed* her to wish me luck. . . . I needed her approval."

Similarly, an artist brought me her paintings from time to time for my reaction. She thought, at first, that it was simply a matter of the pleasure she would derive from my "appreciating" her talent. But it was more than coincidental that she brought in her paintings at those times when she was most troubled, when she most needed my implicit approval to counteract the effect of her own condemning conscience. As she progressed in treatment, she had a dream in which her parents came to see her paintings in a gallery and her mother finally admitted that she *did* have "talent." The triumph was important: her own conscience (with mother as its symbol) was "softening," was becoming less hostile to her self-realization.

While the conscience remains hostile, it is the more necessary to justify one's functioning through assisting others. A brilliant but erratic engineer recalled, for example, that while a student he could never study methodically for a course if he studied alone; but he could, if he had "study buddies"—those he would tutor and help along.

It is not my aim to disparage service to one's fellow. On the contrary, I subscribe to the ancient tenet which holds properly balanced altruism to be no less than "divine." But in those struggling with an overly hostile conscience, this "proper balance" is lost and valid service to oneself unleashes a deluge of anxiety and guilt. In this instance, slavish subservience to the whims and caprices of others can appease the cruel conscience, whereas dropping this defense bares the underlying hatred for the self.

Recurring questions for such a person will be: "How much may I take for *myself?* How much may I *do* for myself?" He will be plagued by these questions and will find himself time and again in the quandary of being unable to decide whether he really has a right to ask for or to accept things that others handle as routine matters. The reasons why these dilemmas recur are "logical." We have seen how the overly harsh conscience fits into the "reason" of such goings on. Now let us develop some additional reasons for the inability to properly "take" for oneself.

We start with the infant in his cradle. It is quite normal that his desires are boundless; and his will is vaguely sensed by him to be omnipotent. In brief, he "reaches for the moon." As he grows—if he develops properly—his desires and will are shaped by reality, so that these gradually become mature and moderate. But if the infant's or child's valid desires are continually and harshly rejected by significant persons, and if his will is unreasonably opposed at every turn, then both tend to be thrust back into the unconscious, and repressed at an early age. Now whatever is repressed tends to remain in the form it had at the time of repression. This means, in this instance, that the repressed desires and urge to power will remain in the unconscious in infantile and primitive formulations.

Therefore, such an individual goes through life plagued by a paradoxical set of things: On the one hand, he generally appears severely inhibited and self-denying regarding his legitimate desires and motives bearing upon self-realization; but occasionally, when generally repressed elements break through, he will express wishes which are so primitive and excessive as to be clearly immature and embarrassing, and he will crave power in such exorbitant measure as to approach the level of omnipotence. In brief, if the individual has not had sufficient opportunity to experience and to express his wishes and desires as he grows, these wishes and desires tend to be perpetuated in infantile form, to be unlimited in scope. The consequence is this conflicting state of things: a) he will want *everything* desirable, without limit; yet b) he will suffer severe anxiety and guilt over requesting or receiving anything at all substantial.

Such a person is apt to worry over whether he is *entitled* to anything, or whether he will be punished for accepting something even when offered. The case comes to mind of a junior executive who received an unusually generous bonus from her employer at the end of the year. Her reaction? Severe anxiety, and a vague pressure of guilt! She recalled, "As a child, whenever I asked for anything, they would say 'Do you really *need* it?' And they almost always proved to me that I could get along without whatever I wished—that I did not *really* need it. . . . Now, I don't know how to demand, and how much not to—because, to be honest—I want to take *everything* for myself. I want so much that it frightens me, and I am afraid to take *anything!*"

This "taking" extends to seeing one's world *for oneself*. Each of us naturally reaches out, to make sense out of his world, to perceive things in the unique way that stamps each an individual. And in such "reaching out," we are often "burned" by parental disapproval. Society has its moral conceptions of what is "right" and "wrong," as well as what is "true" and "false." And even in the best of circumstances, the child will meet at least mild disapproval for investigations, or resulting conclusions, which deviate from society's values. In later years, when the parents' values have been internalized such "reaching out" will often run counter to these values, and thereby incur

disapproval from within. We may generalize thusly:
Knowledge carries its burden of guilt.

This is not alone a medieval devil contract theme: each
of us is in his own way a "Dr. Faustus." For to perceive
clearly and powerfully is to see defects in the authority
figure and in his injunctions. This was exemplified in a
concrete way by a woman struggling to come to grips
with her life problem who came upon this disturbing
insight: "I realize that what makes me feel guilty is that
I seem to be the only one who sees my mother as selfish.
The others pretend that she is just *lovely;* and they are
so very 'sweet'.... But I cannot pretend...."

We may establish this area of hazard to the assumption
of one's full mental powers: the conflict between a) winning acceptance by others, and b) seeing things for
oneself just as clearly as one can. It is not alone a Galileo
who must murmur *"Eppur si muove!"* For when the group
in power believes the earth to be the center of the heavens,
one perceives otherwise at substantial peril. This is particularly true, in an inner sense, where the parent has been
severely competitive and unloving. In such an instance,
the young child must choose between giving up his unfet-
tered powers of perception and creative intelligence, and
losing the acceptance of the all-powerful parent. For the
older child or adult, the second alternative involves—analogously—the supporting function of the conscience, without which he will be plunged into feelings of guilt or
depression.

That is why such people often want the therapist to
support them in their assumption of the ability to see the
truth. One such man would pause characteristically after
each new insight and wait until I commented. He felt so
guilty over seeing things clearly that he became anxious
and depressed if I did not interject some remark implying

my acceptance and approval of his "uncovering." As he progressed and was better able to see the truth, he experienced the following nightmare: "I hear a voice speaking to me. . . . It is the devil, I think. He is saying, 'You are approaching the truth. . . . You are coming very close—and therefore I shall be forced to kill you. I am therefore infusing you with the spirit of dread—and that shall be the end of you!' I feel the spirit inside my body. I feel the most intense anxiety and begin rolling and struggling violently with it. . . . I wake up."

Why was seeing truth so "terrible" a thing? He traced the roots back to his childhood: "My father would always pick on me. . . . The only way I could fight him—I felt —was through 'reason'. . . . So at age ten I sweated through Kant's *Critique of Pure Reason*. . . . And now I have to argue and to defeat in argument those men who remind me of my father. . . . And then, after I defeat them—I feel terribly guilty."

Actually, this sort of guilt-ridden person, when it comes to original or creative thinking, differs from the rest of us only in degree. For creativity involves the "novel." And the novel, running counter to the "established," brings down upon the head of the innovator many painful reminders that humans do not give up old ideas without considerable resentment. For Otto Rank, this was the essence of the Oedipus complex; not a sexual thing, but a "will conflict" between growing individual self-determination and the "counter will of a thousand-year-old moral code. . . . The child must subject himself to it, not in order that he should let his father live and not marry his mother, but that he should not believe in general that he can do what he wishes, that he should not even trust himself to will."

The dreams of persons inordinately involved in such

conflict of wills often manifest their intense guilt over seeing and reporting the truth. Such dreams involve opposing sinister figures whose viciousness betrays the inner understanding that knowledge is dearly bought, that seeing and reporting the truth pose very real threats to one's need for affiliation with and acceptance by the group. We seldom crucify the Philistines of society; it is a fate somehow reserved for those who seek to think and to communicate with honesty.

Social ineptitude may follow directly from guilt. Such an individual ridicules himself before the group, and leads others to offer abuse; he plays the clown and adopts a self-humiliating role. Within his heart is the understanding that he is not a completely worthy "cause"; that he must therefore contribute to his own suffering and curtailed self-realization. It often happens that people at early stages of psychotherapy openly express their emerging resentment in social situations, and consequently suffer social retaliation; whereas later in the process, they experience their resentment *inwardly*, without necessarily letting others know of its existence. Why this difference? The answer seems to be that when the individual can experience his resentment without attendant overwhelming guilt he feels it less necessary to court suffering through such social ineptitude, such imprudent divulging of his hostility.

Chronic vocational failure may also serve to dissipate guilt. We are prone to blame the central causes of vocational failure on external factors and conditions, business slumps, and oppressive competition. More often than is appreciated the essential cause does not reside in these externalities, but rather in an unconscious need for self-punishment. "The ego dares not do certain things because they would bring an advantage and a success which the strict superego has forbidden," is the way Sigmund Freud formulated it. "Thereupon the ego renounces these activities also, in order not to become involved in conflict with the superego." Many of the dramatic "occupational neuroses" appear to belong here, such as writer's and violinist's cramp.

Chronic "bad luck" may be another manifestation. (Karl Menninger refers to "purposive accidents.") The occurrence of so-called accidents among some persons is so fantastically high as to leave little doubt of the existence of an underlying purpose. This purpose is often the temporary ingratiation of oneself with the superego through self-sacrifice and suffering. Such persons are often actively provocative, displaying what Theodor Reik has termed the "provocative factor" in "masochism." They go to great lengths to be imposed upon; they goad others into attacking them for apparently flimsy causes; they play "Russian roulette" with nature, taking chances unnecessarily—and with consequent "accidents." As therapy progressed, a semi-productive writer observed of a recent debacle: "Looking back—I went out of my way to get involved in something like that. . . . I sense a deep-seated urgency to be the target—to get involved, to get into trouble." Dostoevski's burden of guilt, writes Freud in his paper "Dostoevski and Parricide," found relief through his gambling money he could ill afford to lose. "He never rested until he had lost everything. For him gambling was another method of self-punishment. Time after time he gave his young wife his promise or his word of honor not to play any more or not to play any more on that particular day; and as she says, he almost always broke it."

Idealists are highly useful to society, and we owe much of our progress to their altruism. Yet the propensity of some idealistic people to attach themselves to unpopular movements quite certain to bring hardship and misfortune, seriously raises the question of the degree to which their idealism cloaks the immature need to rebel, and the subsequent need to suffer.

Another method, self-effacement, may be employed to the point of chronic self-abuse. Martyrdom may be self-inflicted, and one may bow to any adversary, however puny, and on all issues, however important to the self. The inner understanding is that if one does not stand up for his rights, he shall stand in better stead with his conscience.

Self-humiliation may be useful to the inner self. Never is the child so safe with the competitive parent as when he is "cute" and ineffectual; never so in hazard of rejection as when he manifests maturity and power. The authoritarian conscience, too, patterned after this parent, may be most protective and supportive when the adult invites the world, through his actions, to pity and despise him. However, such unnecessary self-humiliation, we must note, may deeply offend other parts of the self, and engender a self-hatred whose consequences may be severely injurious to evolving selfhood.

Such people as we have here noted find it less threatening to enjoy pleasures under conditions which bring attending pain, or which jeopardize their future. There is sometimes an alternation of pleasure and suffering; the experiencing of a certain amount of suffering apparently gives license for further pleasure. And when, through some twist of fortune, the amount of pleasure substantially exceeds the suffering in any given period, we soon observe these individuals to compensate for this imbalance by flagrant self-destructiveness.

The welcoming of misfortune is frequently observed in psychotherapeutic practice. People in process of analysis, who are making closer contact with their inner world of feelings, report, time and again, their seemingly absurd wish for misfortune. The woman recounting her feelings during a physical examination recalls: "I *wanted* the doctor to tell me that I needed an operation." Another, whose life was running smoothly for the first time in years, reports that she wished a former lover would call—a man who had consistently brought trouble into her life. Similarly, the young executive who had been making steady progress for six months, suddenly suffered strong anxiety along with an exacerbation of symptoms. The cause was that he had been told that very afternoon that he was being groomed for a coveted promotion.

When such persons are creative, they must often work under conditions of discomfort. One could write only when he was severely hungry; another said that he felt "unworthy" of such talent, and that he could only employ that talent when he lived under conditions corresponding to "starving in a garret."

Freud has repeatedly stated that one of the most trying and difficult tasks of psychotherapy is the conquering of a severe unconscious sense of guilt. There is a quantitative factor which enters here: Where relatively few creative functions are inhibited by the sense of guilt, prognosis may not be too poor; but where virtually the person's entire personality is under the control of devastating inhibitions, the condition is considerably less amenable to psychotherapeutic intervention.

Guilt makes for a rigidity of non-creative patterns. The guilt-ridden individual is threatened by the ever alert pressure of inner aggressiveness, and when some insight or incentive leads him to try and escape from self-destructive patterns, this inner pressure tends to slam the door upon his excursion into the world of creative promise. The guilt-ridden individual may therefore be stripped of a positive orientation toward life; of the expectancy of gratification through new experiences; of the inner hope of fruition and fulfillment through meeting and reacting upon life. Instead, severe guilt feelings thrust upon him the necessity for a defensive and negative orientation; his psychological forces and energies must be primarily allocated to holding at bay the guilt feelings which continuously threaten to overwhelm him. He seeks desperately to "get by," rather than to grow—a situation grasped belatedly by a gifted but minimally productive writer, in a moment of insight: "It is true! .... It is true that all my life I have been so occupied with battling my conscience that I could not get *outside*." There is conflict. The will to succeed thrusts obliquely against the guilt over success. Sometimes one force in this conflict is uppermost; sometimes the other. Prolonged hopping from one horn of this dilemma to the other can bring in its wake a profound demoralization, a deep-seated realization of being caught between warring forces, of being on a battleground from which there is no way to escape.

A result of such conflict is often inhibited creative effectiveness. The creative capacities are not entirely relinquished; but then, neither are they entirely free to function. Rather, the level of functioning is somehow felt to be considerably below one's potential. Resentment is therefore directed against those who are felt to be somehow "responsible," as well as those who are not so encumbered, who are relatively free to achieve. This resentment makes for a vicious circle in which anger against the oppressive world adds to the feelings of unworthiness and guilt; and this guilt further increases the required quota of suffering, leading to further inhibition of success, further real failures, and further hostility toward the state of things.

"Why am I so much more guilty than everyone else?" the guilt-ridden individual is apt to ask himself from time to time as he undergoes psychotherapy and comes to better know his feelings. The question may be more in the nature of an accusation: "Why, conscience, do you hate me so relentlessly?"

These questions are more an expression of resentment than of inquiry. The hatred toward authority on the one hand, and toward conscience on the other, add further to the burden of guilt. One young man in treatment expressed it this way: "I feel resentful, and then I feel guilty; and then I feel more resentful over the guilt."

People who are in treatment come to verbalize on this vicious circle. But the actual operation of this interrelationship does not depend upon such verbalization, or even upon awareness. Unconscious hostility may create largely unconscious guilt, and this in turn may provoke further resentment—all with little or no awareness of what is actually taking place. Outbursts of hostility, especially tirades against the parent, may temporarily relieve the tension of resentment, but these soon add to the burden of guilt, and therefore contribute toward the perpetuation of this vicious circle. This is particularly so because the hostility is directed against the very one—the parent—who probably formed the prototype for the individual's authoritarian conscience.

On the other hand, if the individual keeps his hostility strictly repressed, this is no solution either; for the blocking of aggression assists to turn it inward, where it adds to the viciousness of the conscience, and is turned back as a hatred of the self. There is no escape from strong and pervasive unconscious resentment. Such an individual may be chronically ineffectual in life. Flooded continually by hostility and guilt, perhaps provoked periodically by the continuing role of the hypocritical parent, the person may be so continually tense and exhausted from the hostility-guilt-hostility circle as to have little energy or inclination left for constructive effort. "Success" for such a person means "revenge against my parent." One such young man perceived: "The serious thing is—that when it comes to my seeking independence, it is not so much my seeking my own positive development, as it is getting back at my father, who wants me to be forever dependent upon him." Success, therefore, carries a heavy burden of guilt. It means more power to effect hostile intentions. The very abilities which lend themselves to success—the best capabilities in the individual's repertoire—are therefore associated with guilt, and their very use is weighted down with inhibition and depression. One man said: "I wonder why I should feel guilty about every little thing I do for myself. Even writing a number down in my phone book —and I feel guilty!"

Such guilt-laden individuals perform their delinquencies in ways which permit of their being discovered and caught rather easily. In looking back over childhood thefts, one woman observed: "I always did it where I could easily be discovered. . . . I was trying to get everyone to see how bad I was." Quite intelligent adults are by no means immune to this desire. They repeatedly provide illustrations of utter stupidity in the execution of transgressions against authority's injunctions; their ineptitude serves to effect self-defeat and subsequent reparation. Where there is severe unconscious hostility, power implies "power for evil"—for aggression against authority, and against the conscience molded in the form of that authority. Hence, self-defeat serves to avoid further guilt.

Where there is guilt there will be a need to suffer. And where there is a need to suffer innate intelligence will be perverted from creative goals, and deflected toward a habitual fabrication of pits and snares for self-entrapment and self-hurt.

VIII

THE QUEST FOR SIGNIFICANCE

An enormous and tragic blind spot of our time is the persistence of the superficial and erroneous understanding that every human being necessarily seeks his own best interests. Though we may be sophisticated in the physical sciences, we generally cling to the puerile belief that intelligent people necessarily intelligently seek what is best for themselves. Contrastingly, clinical study clearly reveals the existence of a duality of paths. Each of can "adjust," that is, can defend himself against painful feelings, either through constructive and creative effort or through clearly and often monstrously self-destructive approaches to the problems of life. Why should such goings on exist? —whatever happened in the past to bring forth such monstrous behavior?

The answer, time and again, has to do with the crucial developmental years; the parent repeatedly wounded the child's self-esteem, and wounded it so badly that the young one developed "poor" habits of behavior and unfortunate techniques for "grasping at straws" in order to maintain a shred of a sense of personal significance.

Such parents are often "too close" to the child in a peculiar, but important sense; they are likely to be perfectionistic, and to subject the child's behavior to the same microscopic examination they habitually give their own. Such a parent is inclined to see the child as an extension of her own ego, and therefore to "hound" him in the same way in which she has been hounding *herself* through the years.

I remember seeing a woman walking her toddling infant on the street, some months ago. He gazed in fascination at a gaily colored pole on the sidewalk, upon which his mother pointed to it and said gravely, "Barber pole!" He dutifully mimicked, "Baba poe," and happily prepared to toddle on. But she held him still as she said sternly *"Bar-ber pole."* His reply again was "Baba poe." Obviously displeased, she permitted him to move on. I sighed as I saw what was going on, for many of the serious self-defeating patterns I see at the clinic are traceable to essentially this sort of repeated exposure to carping parental criticism. The child will probably learn that he cannot discover the "barber poles" of life by himself. Rather, mother will interject herself between him and his world, and since mother is compulsively critical and perfectionistic he will probably learn that no amount of trying will really please her. Whether it is a case of pronouncing "barber pole," getting grades at school, or learning the social graces, such a parent is apt to leave the impression with the child that he is simply not doing well enough. I admit that if the child happens to be a genius he might really satisfy such parents. But for the rest of us, for merely "bright" people, such parents provide repeated heartache. They are usually overly competitive, and push their children toward being outstanding scholars —when they are yet in grade school. And the child soon learns: "It's no use. It's impossible to really please them. No matter what I get, they want more!—If I get an 80, they want 85 . . . If 85, they want 95."

This sort of rejection—however unintentional—is an intense cruelty. It can assume vicious proportions, for the issue at stake is the parent's own ego. When the child fails to achieve the brilliance the parent craves from her ego extension he suffers the same sort of cold scorn the parent really harbors for herself. She would hardly be as cruel to a neighbor's child, for there she is not "involved" and maintains perspective. But she is capable of unwittingly wounding her own child's sense of significance repeatedly, and on a very deep level.

Pathetic indeed are the stories some self-defeatists tell of how as children, they tried, year after year, to earn their parents' acceptance. One man recalled that when he played basketball in the neighborhood schoolyard and his father drove by, he would shoot the ball one-handed from wherever he was, hoping desperately that he would make a goal *when his father could see it,* so that he could feel accepted and loved, if just for a moment. With the passage of years, such a child becomes conditioned to expect painful rejection whenever he wholeheartedly tries to apply himself to doing the very best he can. He learns: "It's no use. No matter how I try—they're always going to tell me 'It's not good enough!' " He therefore becomes conditioned to feeling worthless—whenever faced with a task requiring wholehearted effort.

The basketball player, grown to self-defeating manhood, tried to start his own business, but was flooded with depression. He reported: "I have over three thousand leads to people who bought this product [a house appliance] ten years or so ago, and who should be ready to buy a new one. But I feel so discouraged. . . . I feel I will

fail. . . . I feel 'What's the use?' . . . I can't believe in
my own capabilities. If someone says 'You're great!' I can
walk around on a cloud for weeks. . . . But if no one says
I'm 'great' then I feel I'm 'terrible.' " Several years earlier
he had tried to sell mutual funds, but became discouraged.
"When I had a presentation to make," he said, "I always
feared that the person I faced would know more about
mutual funds that I did. . . . But that was absurd! If he
knew *that* much he wouldn't be asking me for a presentation. . . . Why do I feel inferior?" he continued. "I just
can't reason *why* I should continually criticize myself.
Why do I always expect failure? Why don't I look for
success?"

But the feelings of inadequacy persisted. How could it
be otherwise when his father had consistently criticized him
at every turn, had shown him in a thousand ways that
he, the father, could do everything "better"? Such parents
later have reason to regret what they have done. "Richard
is a defeatist. . . . He gives in too quickly," reported one
such parent in a moment of insight. But let us further advance the insight: Richard is not only *defeating* himself—he
is also *defending* himself; defending himself against the
terrible anxiety associated with "trying again," defending
himself by not *really* trying any more.

I'm sure the reader knows of underachievers of this sort,
for I see them very often in clinical practice. They once
tried to do their very best, but now give no more than
halfhearted effort to anything. They are often very bright
young people, potentially capable of high level work; but
they coast along on far lower levels of achievement. They
usually don't know why: "The teacher's no good," or
"I just don't care for school," may be the kinds of reasons
that come to their minds. In fact, they are defending their
self-concepts, and avoiding feelings of unworthiness by
side-stepping any real test of what they can do. If they

don't really try, if they don't do their lessons and their homework, then they might be called "lazy" and "delinquent"; but the possibility is still open that if they *did* try they might yet be the high level geniuses their parents crave.

In such a household, it is far less painful—in terms of the terrible and deep anxiety we suffer when we feel insignificant—to be a "delinquent and lazy genius in the rough" than to be a conscientious "mediocrity," since the "delinquent" is spoken to by the hopeful perfectionist parent who admonishes, pleads, threatens, cajoles, somewhat like this: "My boy, I *know* you can do it! You're a chip off the old block. All you have to do is try and you'll cover us all with glory. I just know you can live up to what I had hoped I myself would become. So, until the next lecture, go in and try!" So life goes on, with the "delinquent" still the apple of his competitive father's eye.

But if our bright youngster *really* continues to apply himself wholeheartedly, he comes to find the perfectionist parent regarding him with what one such boy termed a "fishy stare." There is no room in such a family for mere "brightness." Such parents regard it as mediocrity, and direct largely unconscious hatred and contempt toward the child, even as they direct these feelings toward themselves. In our competitive society, we tend to "love" our children in the same way we love ourselves: that is, with goodly measures of contempt and hatred for our deviations from idealized self-concepts.

So it often happens that a child grows up with a deficient sense of his own significance. As we have seen, such a child may defend himself from such feelings of unworthiness by self-defeating underachieving, which happens to be a common form of self-defeat in the current scene.

There are additional important forms of self-defeating

defenses against such feelings of insignificance. One is to feud "senselessly" with parents and their substitutes—teachers, employers, and so on. The purpose is analogous to this: "I upset the court's verdict of my 'badness' by proving the judge *himself* to be 'bad.'" Such people have a need to interminably cross swords with the meaningful people in their lives. One man said of his authoritarian wife: "Something inside me wants to hate her. . . . I don't understand why. . . . I really don't *want* to understand why. . . . I only know that I get such pleasure out of hating." And he reported in regard to various employers: "In my daydreams, I used to conjure up situations in which someone would accuse me of something, and I would defend myself."

In order to appreciate the vehemence of this feud, one must see it in terms of *the sense of personal significance.* The parent had so often—and deeply—implied the child's basic insignificance and lack of goodness that the issue for the later adult has become one of emancipation from this unbearable, deeply etched slur. The formula for freedom is this: "I can vindicate myself, I can prove my goodness, only by condemning my judge of childhood, only by overwhelming proof of this parent-judge's essential corruption and unworthiness." In this light, we can understand why it is far more important for the adult to prove the figure of authority "bad" than to succeed at something needed for his own self-realization. This is the sort of compulsion the psychiatrist Edmund Bergler refers to in terms of the individual's seeking "'proof' of the mother's evilness."

One such man became aware that he did not take notes in an important training class because he was ambivalent as to whether he wanted to succeed at all. "If I succeed my mother would be sure to crow about it—to take credit for it." He had a deep need to confront his mother with the very opposite state of affairs—to fill her eyes day after day with the proof of how irretrievably she had *wrecked* him.

The basic issue in this fight is over the sense of personal goodness and significance. The competitive or insufficiently loving parent injured this sense, either through derogation or through failing to grant sufficient signs of love. The child, and eventuating adult, indulge in this fight so as to lift the burden of "badness," of insignificance, from *their* selves, and to place it squarely upon the parent. As we mature, we develop many ways by which to support the sense of significance: our careers, the clubs we join, self-cultivation, and so on. But as young children, we depend quite exclusively upon the attention and acceptance our parents show us. And parents who are preoccupied with other things wound the child's basic sense of worthiness in very consequential ways.

One self-defeating man recalled that his father—seven days a week—spent practically all his waking hours with the prize fighters he managed. The *central* urge of the young man's developing life became a need to prove that his father didn't spend time with him, not because *he* didn't deserve it, but because his father was a "louse." He therefore employed a tried and true mechanism for proving his father's "lousehood": "I get hurt and it's *his* fault!"

This is the mechanism used in many varieties of self-destructive behavior such as chronic alcoholism, gambling, and overeating. This was exemplified in a minor way by a self-defeatist who spent an entire session talking about trivia, and consciously avoiding material he knew to be important; at the very end of the session he blurted out, "Look! I wasted the whole session!" and he glared at me reproachfully. This man also "could not" enjoy life. He had an attractive wife, a good career, excellent physical health but enjoyed none of these. He just couldn't. He *mustn't*. It would be too much of a vindication of his mother whom he simply *had* to condemn. If he enjoyed life it would mean that she had not been "bad," and had given him an adequate upbringing; if she were not bad, then the inescapable conclusion would be that she neglected him in childhood simply because *he* was not worthy.

Such a man may court abuse. He may seek his own misfortune to prove the badness of his parent. The unhappy instance comes to mind of the teen-age boy who broke into a stationery store, ostensibly because he needed a fountain pen to do his school work and did not want to ask his father (who had rejected him quite roundly) for anything at all. But here is the point: Had he picked up a pen and left after breaking into the store, he probably would not have been caught. Instead, he "shopped around" inside the store for a full half-hour, collecting various non-essential school supplies, and was easily apprehended by the policeman making his rounds. The boy eventually came to appreciate that he wanted to be caught so that the entire community could know that his father's indifference, his father's badness, had driven him to such an involvement. Note the extent of his self-abusive efforts: "When the police came I tried to run away. . . . They caught me. . . . I fought. They clubbed me pretty bad. . . . I asked them to shoot me!"

Such people inflict severe suffering upon themselves so that they can blame the unloving parent. One accident-prone laboratory technician who had burned herself quite severely in the latest "accident" continually held up her bandaged hand as a badge of her suffering at the hands of the world (a world which had largely assumed the place of her egotistical father). It is rather shocking, even to the experienced clinician, to observe a badly burned person who displays her wounds with quite obvious pleasure and triumph in her eyes. One begins to doubt oneself and the ability to recognize emotions, except for a number of complementary features, such as 1) the patient's own understandings develop along the same lines, 2) a relatively integrated dynamic picture emerges, into which this paradox fits cogently, 3) improvement in the patient's freedom to behave creatively tends to accompany and to follow such emerging insights, and 4) observations of other clinicians corroborate one's own. The need to feel basically worthwhile *is* so vital that people will harm themselves in order to "set the record straight"—to accuse the unloving parent and his surrogates of a lack of goodness.

Such a person may engage in what is termed "malevolent transformation." Since he unconsciously desires to perceive others as unloving and heartless, he may actually goad and provoke them (including the reasonably kind ones) to behave in ways which appear selfish, cruel, and malevolent. "When it happens that authority *can* be a bastard," one such man said, "I sort of hope it will be—so I can hate it." And he did what he could to help this process along. This is one of the main reasons why some people defeat themselves during psychotherapy. They have such a strong urge to perceive the therapist as an "enemy" that they actually goad him toward being irritated and eventually "fed up" with them—sometimes to the point of actual rejection.

Women like this may be markedly seductive, continually tempting the therapist to "prove" that he really cannot be trusted after all. Men with this urge are no less provoking: As one young man put it, "I feel it's absolutely essential to distort—to transform you from Dr. Samuel Warner to Mr. John Jones" (his father)—"and then to *fight* you."

Such individuals provoke interested teachers to outright

rejection, cooperative business partners and colleagues to blunt antagonism, and initially loving wives or husbands to becoming petulant discontents; they devote so much ingenuity and energy to fighting, and provoking retaliation, as to preclude the possibility of possessing the energy and inclination for fully living life. Only later, when psychotherapy has brought the person closer to his underlying feelings, does he consciously identify and experience the unrelenting rage which perpetuates his feud with ubiquitous parental figures. As he explored the reasons for protracted self-destructive feuds with employers, a young executive fumed: "All through the years they've kicked me. And now they want to be nice to me. The devil with that! . . . I don't want them to be vindicated by their petty peace offerings." Such a man opposes authority in every possible way. Karen Horney formulated this phenomenon in the therapeutic context: Such a person finds it inwardly "more important to defeat the efforts or to thwart the possible success of the teacher or physician" than to succeed himself.

It is a "kiss of death" for any project if such an individual's parent expresses approval of it. The spice and interest in *any* activity, for these people, resides largely in its potential for opposing parental wishes, for venting the steadily erupting resentment. If the parent learns about an activity and expresses approval of it, then, as one teen-ager reported, as he suddenly dropped plans he had made with early enthusiasm: "I would only be doing what she *expects* of me."

The phrase "injustice collector," coined by Dr. Bergler, well describes such self-defeatists. The collector goes to extremes of self-defeat in order to suffer visibly, to suffer under the obvious "cruelty" and "injustice" perpetrated by an authority figure. As treatment progresses, such collectors become increasingly aware of their wish to be refused. One young woman realized that when she waited on line to register for college courses, she faintly hoped that a particular section of a desired course would be filled, and therefore closed, before she could reach the registration window. This would have permitted the temporary experiencing of the "disinterest" and "cruelty" of the parent surrogates.

This urge to collect injustices is often gratified in marriage. As one man told of the pressure being exerted by his wife to "keep up with the Joneses" beyond what they could safely afford, he smiled faintly. Why the smile at such a time? Quite surely—because he derived satisfaction from her driving him toward difficulty. Such an individual may be quite active in provoking "malevolence"; and when he is finally refused, he inwardly wins a victory in his struggle and says covertly, at such time—in another excellent phrase provided by Dr. Bergler—"Bad mother refuses!"

In the therapeutic situation, the inwardly hostile patient may go to near-bizarre extremes to push the therapist into the role of the "bad mother" who refuses him love. I recall one young man who planted his feet squarely on my desk during our first interview, doodled on my desk pad, and, as the session neared its close, brusquely demanded the loan of a small amount of money. This young man had gone through nine therapists, and had succeeded in transforming each into a "bad mother" who wanted little more of the patient than that he remove himself. Subsequently, this man turned out to be a highly responsive and successful patient; but this happy turn of events took place only after repeated honest communication on the subject of his provocative maneuvers. Along the way, he reached this insight: "I tease you—until you reach the breaking point and storm at me. . . . And then I am *shocked!*" But a subtlety of his injustice collecting lay in this: A "good" therapist, he believed, would never display such a "breaking point." Even when wearing the sackcloth and ashes of contrition, he still cast me in the role of the "bad one."

This fight against parent surrogates is carried on without the self-defeatist's awareness of what he is really doing; he finds it extremely difficult to cooperate with figures of authority, even when such cooperation is crucially in his own interest. It is as if a point of "honor" were involved. To cooperate carries for such people a deep sense of repugnance. To cooperate is to "give in," to "make up," in a situation where self-respect can be nurtured only through a continuing fight. As one man came to see it: "I want to hang on to my grudge. . . . It is as if authority says 'You are no good!'. . . So you must prove authority to be wrong in everything." Were he to find it possible to get along with authority, this would mean a vindication of the "tyrant." Far better to find it impossible, so to retain the inner image of the parent surrogate. One's spouse may readily substitute. A young wife, for example, who had long complained about her husband's not earning enough, came at one point to this startling insight: "You know—I think that I really don't *want* Jim to make more money. . . . I think that I make things happen so as to have a logical basis for my hostility. . . . I want to say: 'See what sort of position *you* have put me into!' "

One can preserve one's sense of personal goodness and significance through engineering one's own rejection. If one feels deeply and essentially unworthy ("my wormhood," as one man phrased it), if one feels it to be only a matter of time before others discover how "bad," unlovable, and unworthy one is, if one feels it to be only a matter of time before one is rejected, then it may serve one's self-esteem to *do* something, to give cause for rejection, rather than to wait until the rejection arrives in due course. For if one provides a specific act which forms the basis for rejection, then one can feel *that act* is to blame; which is much easier to bear than feeling that "no matter *what* one does, one is so unacceptable as to be rejected anyway." In this context, actively provocative self-defeating acts serve a defensive role for self-esteem.

Such patients try the therapist's patience. Always anxious over what they sense to be imminent and inevitable rejection, they continually provoke the therapist to terminate their treatment. They repeatedly annoy him and overstep the few realistic restrictions imposed upon their freedom in the therapeutic relationship so as to force the therapist's hand. "Better to end treatment on the basis of a particular breach of agreement," they inwardly feel, "than to be 'eased out' anyway, because the doctor has no interest in working with me."

Analogous behavior is found, as we have seen, in other varieties of relationships, as in marriage, where a wife will nag and annoy until her husband bellows rejection over the endless irritation; after which there is a period of calmed relief. She is relieved when his fury is aimed at something she has actually done. By bringing his anger down upon her head over picayune harping on some inconsequential thing, she feels that she has put off the day when he not only will reject some specific instance of nagging, but will reject her entirely. Some marriages are therefore characterized by the game: "Blame, blame! . . . Who's got the blame?" For a spouse may simply *have* to feel her mate is in the wrong if she can feel at all "right." As one woman came to see it: "It is as if my husband is in the wrong, or *I* am in the wrong. . . . One of us has *got* to be wrong."

In the work situation, the same sorts of forces make for

a running on-the-job "war." For, though generally unable
to verbalize the underlying meaning, the person involved
nevertheless senses authority figures to be working against
his own best interests, and therefore feels impelled to
oppose them. His work history will therefore be marred by
repeated failure to profit from extended opportunities, or
by repeated loss of positions he could easily have held to
advantage. He inwardly interprets cooperating with an
employer as "giving in," and losing an important "battle."
To such individuals (who had long suffered hurt and humiliation at the hands of demanding parents) work itself
is felt to be a deep insult to one's dignity; these people
carry a grudge against figures of authority, and work represents a capitulation to the "tyrant" or his surrogate. One
man who had repeatedly experienced considerable difficulty in finding and in keeping suitable employment remarked during therapy: "I don't know why, but just
getting a job in itself feels like a betrayal of something
precious within me. . . . And when I'm working, when I
think of how much money my boss is making off my
services, I really get tied up in knots." A gifted writer who
continually ruined opportunities for selling his work came
eventually to perceive that for him, it was a personal war
against those who were established, those set up to make
money through his work. Even though he would also benefit from publication, it was like "giving in." And he hated
to give in. "I can see where I provoke them into reacting in
a punishing way toward me," said the writer. "In that way
I can hate the publishing situation even more."

They destroy their own opportunities for succeeding, as
part of their campaign to make the charge of malevolence
more convincing. I am reminded of the bright young
lawyer, who, upon obtaining a desirable position with a
sedate law firm, was warned to conduct and dress himself

in a manner consistent with the organization's reputation for dignity. It was hardly chance that led him to wear flamboyant sports clothes to the office, and to behave without decorum: reasons for his early dismissal. The loss was a serious one for his career, and for some time later he refused to perceive his own role in forcing his dismissal; on the contrary, during this time, he complained about the heartlessness of the officers in cutting short his employment for such "petty" reasons.

Such people sometimes goad others into a retaliatory sitdown of their own. The instance comes to mind of the young businessman who reported—with a display of righteous indignation—the chronic lateness shown by his partner in arriving for work each morning. "This is very bad, very bad indeed," he murmured, wondering aloud how long a man could stay in business if his partner took so little interest in affairs. It was only after considerable time in treatment that the more complete truth emerged. The partner had initially been extremely conscientious, perhaps overly so, whereas the patient himself had for years been thoroughly disinterested, characteristically arriving for work near noon and leaving early. It had only been after some years of pleading—to no avail—that the conscientious partner became demoralized, and began arriving late himself. And *then* the patient changed! Becoming a paragon of middle-class virtue, he set an example at work, showing to all the world how wretchedly he suffered at the hands of his faithless partner! This was where his account began.

Such feuding takes the place of actual functioning; long drawn-out complaining takes the place of actual living. One's marriage, one's career, one's life itself are turned from the quest for self-realization and toward the goal of proving others to be bad, unfaithful, and untrustworthy.

Thus, the quest for significance leads inexorably to the spoiling of whatever chances one has for really enjoying life, and for truly fulfilling oneself, leading one man to sadly realize, "Somehow I get the feeling that I've lost a lot of time in life—that I really haven't used my brain fully, that I haven't been digging into things the way I should."

To which we may add that his "brain" had indeed been used, but largely to an ill-directed end. A gnawing sense of insignificance, born of past chronic insult to self-esteem, had through the years pressured him into the frantic use of self-defeating modes to achieve a sense of significance. As Bacon noted: "They do but trifle with themselves that labour in past matters."

IX

SIGNIFICANCE AND THE
CREATIVE APPROACH

Damage to one's sense of significance can undermine the creative approach to life. Insults to what one feels one *should* be can produce a wasteland of the potentially creative self. Let us continue with our discussion of the mechanisms whereby one's need for significance works for self-defeat; let us see how creativity shrivels and dies in a climate of disparagement.

"When I was eleven or so," a young man recalled, "I decided to take up photography. My father bought me an expensive camera, and fine equipment. . . . I had a dark room. . . . It cost my father, all told, close to five hundred dollars. But he came in one day to show me how to develop pictures—to develop them 'right' (as he would say) . . . . And from that day on, I never went into the dark room again. . . . I had electric trains. But he *showed* me how to play with the trains. And I never played with them again. . . . There was a certain insincerity about my father. When he 'taught' me—he was really showing me what a great guy he was. He'd pick on everything I did. Nothing was 'good enough'. . . . I wanted so badly to show him I *was* good enough. I wanted to develop pictures he would praise me for. But fat chance! . . . So now, the only reason why I want to succeed is to show him I *can* make it big. But if I can't make it big then I don't feel like trying at all."

And he did *not* try any more. His very considerable talents lay rotting—and I mean that literally: for a mind not used tends to regress and fall apart, like timber on a vessel not properly utilized and cared for. He went through the motions of living. But his creative capacities, the urges and powers to perceive new and better paths toward making the most of his life, were shunted aside as if they did not exist at all.

The disparaging parent had wounded the man's self-esteem long before; but the self-defeating mechanisms of defense continued to operate long afterwards. The need to make a "big splash," or else nothing at all, undermines the opportunities for moving ahead creatively—be it in the arts, sciences, or business world.

The functioning premise involved is this: "I must be outstanding. I must not be 'merely' successful—I must be an *outstanding* success!"

How "outstanding" a success would satisfy the self-defeatist? What degree of success would permit him to function or to complete his creative task? When you ask him, his reply is vague. He actually does not know. He knows only that he is driven, that he has been driven all his life, to achieve a most "stupendous" success. And if he cannot achieve that, then he would rather drop the whole thing, and default.

"Why is it," he continued, "whenever something is going a little bit right I try to kill it! . . . Like the first day out with the line—yesterday—I got two big orders. . . .

So you know what I did today? I took the line out and I went to the movies! . . . I don't know why I did it. It's like somebody was pulling me with a string." But he dug deeper into his associations, and came up with reasons. "I've got to be either *very* good, or *very* bad. I can't be a plain ordinary success. I've got to be either very good —or a bust! . . . I'm afraid of being mediocre. Because nobody cares about a mediocre person. Nobody talks about a mediocre person. . . . It's the same way when I dress. I've got to be either terrifically 'dressed up' or sloppy. . . . I guess I compare myself with other people who are a *big* success. And when I start to be a success, but feel I can't be as successful as this one or that one, then I don't try any more. . . . Then I make a mockery of whatever I'm doing. It becomes a humorous situation for me. I know it's a sucker's game to go for an inside straight. But I go for it every time because I feel that if I *got* that 'six of clubs' I would feel like a *big* man!"

And thus, a peculiar bipolarity comes into existence. The one with injured self-esteem often feels that he must be outstanding: either an outstanding success, or an outstanding failure—but he must be deviant, and he must be deviant by his own hand. He cannot content himself with ordinary success, success in keeping with his actual level of competence. Such success is for him "mediocrity," which he abhors more intensely than abject self-determined failure. He would rather be sporadically unemployed than work steadily at a fairly good position which would, in time, stamp him as adequately competent, but not a genius.

To the man who harbors chronic resentment toward authority, who inwardly nurses an injured self-concept, and who renders each day bearable by dosage with the opiate of future grandiosity, there is little or no pride in being an "average success." There is rather capitulation to the competitive parent who had continually disparaged and insulted, and implied that he alone was admirable and effectual. There is for this man a sense of significance only in extremes; in the actual achievement of outstanding success, or in chronic—albeit self-engineered—outstanding failure. The first demonstrates to the parent that his much-disparaged offspring possesses gifts which exceed his own; the second punishes the parent by humiliating him.

Therefore, in those of deeply injured self-esteem, we repeatedly see this pattern: They begin a project by energetically aiming for tremendous success; falling short of this, they turn aside from attainable success, and plunge to abysmal failure. This pattern is repeated so often as to rule out the role of accident.

One such man had a fantastically poor college record whereas he could easily have earned a "B" average on the basis of his intelligence quotient. His pattern was this: At the start of a course he would begin ambitiously, and do fairly well on the first examination. But "fairly well" was not the genius-level success he craved. He therefore lost interest in succeeding in *usual* ways, took few examinations, failed to submit final papers—and, by hook or by crook, managed to eke out a passing grade by manipulating the instructor's sympathies. Better acquainted with the Dean's office than with the library, this man was graduated with the lowest possible point average. He suspects, and possibly with good reason, that the Dean "threw a few points onto the scale" at the end, to get rid of him. And all this with an unquestionably superior intellect!

Although he began each school term with the resolve to submit assignments promptly, tensions began to mount progressively as he worked, and soon assumed unbearable proportions. The inner understanding was: "You will only find rejection, and anxiety, and depression if you go ahead and submit the fruits of your best creative labor. Don't be deceived into believing that top-level functioning will bring the acceptance and sense of significance you crave. You have already had ample experiences in the past to establish beyond doubt that betrayal and humiliation await the submission of conscientious work. Find some *other* way to feel significant!"

Thus, the craving for significance can lead to an ominous bipolarity, a tendency toward either of two extreme positions. In spite of a conscious wish for self-realization, a man may present this ultimatum to the world—which, in effect, adamantly links the need to be "outstanding" with self-defeat: "My price for cooperating with you—O world!—is grandiose status. Either you grant it to me in the realm of success, or I will seize it by default—as a mystifying but enormous chronic failure!" Unfortunately, one of these alternatives is considerably more likely to eventuate than the other.

There are additional facets to the influence of the disparaging household. One must give of oneself in order to partake of the creative process; but the unloving household exposes the child to the constant fear of being unfairly criticized, ridiculed, and shamed. Therefore, the human product of such a household becomes anxious when he is "different" in any way, and unconsciously tends to inhibit this process.

Such a person fears being spontaneous. He cannot expose the products of selfhood to the eyes of others. And since novelty is essential to the creative unfolding of the self's possibilities, he represses the inner richness of his being, and embraces instead only those areas of his inner life which readily fit the socially "safe" cliché. Here, the urge toward self-realization falls prey to the untoward need for acceptance by significant figures of the social scene.

He is apt to be filled with pent-up resentment, and this

further interferes with his potential for communicating with his inner world; for if one permits oneself to know one's own heart, one will surely often think critically about others. But the man who is filled with resentment is reluctant to experience such critical thoughts, fearing they may manifest an inner generalized bitterness, rather than valid criticism. He fears his own impulses, and fears knowing himself, lest the very awareness of socially unacceptable impulses somehow outwardly betray their existence. He fears, as well, truly communicating with others lest this reveal what is actually going on within himself. He therefore tends toward minimal knowledge of himself, and defensive dissimulation with others; these blocks to fluency produce not only a wary and secretive attitude which reduces communication but also a constricted approach to his inner life which severely penalizes the unfolding of his potentials.

One such man had a dream which clearly revealed why he was so inwardly blocked from moving ahead: Getting ahead and succeeding meant "getting even" with his disparaging father. And "showing up" the man whom one had loved and feared for so long was indeed something frightful, and to be avoided. Yet a sense of significance was demanded by the heart. Where self-esteem is damaged, destructiveness is bound to be unleashed, to attack whatever is "bad," whatever is not "significant." And therefore this man turned from a creative approach to life. He found his significance—strange as it may at first seem—through self-defeat.

For, under prolonged exposure to insults, under chronic offense to self-concept, the burning issue becomes—avoidance of further humiliation, rather than positive movement toward self-realization. One chronically self-defeating man reported, in a moment of insight: "Whether I succeed or

not is for me a side-issue: I am not accustomed to succeed. . . . But what I *must* keep myself from doing is bending the knee and crawling—humiliating myself in front of
people."

And what way is more available for avoiding "bending
the knee and crawling" than—simply *opposing?* If a child
feels chronically humiliated by an overbearing and disparaging parent what readier opposition is there than simply
not doing one's lessons, not getting out of bed on time in
the morning, not taking adequate care of personal property? The poor or failing report card will surely underline the fact that the child is a force to be reckoned with
in the household. The parent can count on very little peace
of mind when the child casually "overlooks" doing what is
expected of him—and, of course, defeats himself at the
same time.

If the growing child's self-concept is sufficiently insulted, the craving for self-esteem may be so intense as to
foster a rigid adherence to whatever mechanisms are immediately efficacious. Where such functioning mechanisms
involve the primitive sense of power, and where self-and-
other defeating tactics have become habituated as modes
of achieving this sense of power, the prognosis for creative
personality growth may be guarded indeed. Creative effort
may take considerable time, whereas self-and-other defeat
is quite immediate; and when underlying anxiety and depression seep through, such a child (and later adult) are
prone to quickly call forth the defense mechanisms which
have been known to function effectively in the past, such
as the sense of power through self-and-other defeat, and
to persist rigidly in the employment of such self-destructive
opiates.

The destructive parent, teacher, or supervisor may so
condition the individual to expect ridicule when he seeks

to create as to cause the very act of creation to be associated with feelings of injured self-esteem. The rigidly destructive supervisor may sustain his own sense of significance through systematically discouraging and subtly disparaging a subordinate, a situation not uncommon among persons in positions of power within a bureaucratic structure. Protracted pressures of this sort may wreak havoc upon the creativity of the younger man. For insults to self-esteem, however subtle, tend to be cumulative and to mount in pressure; and since these proddings are associated with seeking to cooperate and to produce creatively, the younger man's heart may break, so to speak, and he may completely turn against his urge to create. He may regress to primitive formulations of the quest for power as solace for the sense of significance, and may therefore cease cooperating on the job, or cease utilizing his full creative potential, so as to strike back at the supervisor and at the job situation associated with these repeated and protracted insults to self-concept, and so to sense power by virtue of his ability *to oppose*.

Where the job situation is in a large organization, and relatively "secure," he may be loath to leave it because of his years of seniority; so he stays on, year after year, in an employment setting where he is dedicated to opposing the one above him (and, by extension, the entire organization), and where he strongly resists the full use of his creative capacities for constructive effort. Such a person will shuffle his way through his work, although he has the ability to move far more energetically. The need to frustrate the supervisor and the organization comes to undermine the urge to make the most of himself. The immediate and continual need for sustenance to self-esteem comes to take precedence over long term requirements for self-realization. His creative efforts are characterized by a chronic slow-down, which serves the need for a sense of significance through power, and this need is fed by the passive-aggressive "inability" to work as quickly, or to think as creatively, as his innate potentials might otherwise permit.

The "pushing parent" has a similar effect by being overly eager that the child "accomplish" things. School grades must be higher, piano practice periods must be extended to speed accomplishment, grace is not being sufficiently acquired at ballet class, and so on. Such pressure generally manifests less a love for the child than it does egocentricity in the parent: neurotic competitiveness expressed through the child-appendage. Such pressure does not assist self-realization; it hampers it. Both the parent and the superego fashioned after this parent will operate in such a way as to place a severe strain upon the child (and subsequent adult), to impose an oppressive and chronic tension on him over fear of failure. The child whose life is implicitly dedicated to the neurotic glory of the parent is the one who will be prone to condemnation by his severe conscience over any display of imperfection or "weakness" in the context of the parent's exorbitant demands. Such a conscience will storm and rage at the hapless one who "fails"; will withdraw its support of self-esteem when temporary reversals are met; will provide its marginal support only when parental neurotic demands are being satisfied; and will viciously condemn the self when not. Such condemnation by the conscience for ordinary human limitations or failings will tend to set up rigid defenses against the consequent anxiety and guilt. It will make for rigid boundaries in the inner mental life, and for pained caution in thought and feeling—for one must be cautious in seeking to develop one's potentials if the consequences of less than top level success are so lastingly agonizing.

In brief, the "pushing" parent, who does not love the

child for itself, but only for its unusual accomplishments, does not generally push the child in a creative direction, but rather toward an oversensitivity to possible failure, and a timidity which breeds a prolonged succession of *actual* failures. In time, these failures undermine the morale. One hardly dares try any more to accomplish anything. At the beginning of a project, one such man characteristically started with the frenzied energy of desperation. He could not work for *future* gain, for he had little faith in his ability to achieve a distant goal. Instead, he clutched prematurely and shortsightedly at immediate results, and was accordingly brusque, argumentative, and complaining in the face of the usual obstacles, alienating those whose good will he needed for succeeding. He said of fairly ordinary frustrations: "These things all get into my guts, and they frighten me." Indeed, these minor trials did frighten him. But the buzzing of a mosquito would be frightening too if one were perched on a tightrope over Niagara Falls. To a fugitive from feelings of worthlessness, the potential plunge downward is into a very deep and dark abyss of insignificance.

Such people doggedly avoid tests of who they are, and of what they can do. A highly qualified salesman avoided looking for a job for a full year. As he explained it, "What will happen to me, if I try again—and fail?" He answered the question for himself: "I'll get worse!"

To his family and friends he appeared "lazy," as for months on end—after being fired from his previous job— he did little more than eat and sleep. But he himself came to know how very essential it was to keep his image of himself from deteriorating any further: "I mustn't fail," he said. "I don't mind people saying 'You're lazy!' But it's *terrible* to be a *'failure'*!"

He was personable and likable. His friends set up interviews for him with influential people who could readily offer him good positions, but he discouraged their efforts. He just couldn't, for the time being, subject his self-concept to any further "injury"; he was suffering too much anxiety. For his last position—culminating in his dismissal—had been the straw that broke the back of his morale.

It is true that with his self-defeating opposition and power maneuvers he had set things up so that there was really no alternative to his being fired. Yet he had shielded himself from the knowledge of his self-defeating nuisance operations, and knew only that somehow another, and this time overwhelming, defeat had been encountered. Now he lived by a simple but devastating defensive logic, which he eventually came to perceive on his own: "If I don't try—then I can't fail."

That is the way it spirals. The disparaging parent sets the stage for the development of a "delicate ego," a fragile self-concept characterized by insufficient self-esteem. Next, the child develops self-and-other defeating ways of nurturing his sense of significance. Third, the developing child and young man employ these sick ways through the years, and amass a record of defeat in school and at work. These defeats then threaten even more his sense of significance, causing repetitions of the vicious circle of self-and-other defeat: The culmination is a "breakdown" of some sort. The man under discussion sensed well that trying again, that seeking to achieve, would arouse further anxiety. For to seek to achieve is to *hope*, to anticipate a future fruition. And this is the point: To hope—to open one's anticipations to the possibility of fulfillment in the future—is to expose oneself to further anxiety. This is part of the mechanism of psychological depression; depression serves as a defense against anxiety. Clinical work with depressed people underlines their reluctance to hope again;

for the state of hopefulness exposes them to intense anxiety.

This is not a modern insight. Seneca perceived it nineteen centuries ago: "Just as the same chain holds both the prisoner and his guard, so hope and fear, dissimilar as they are, march linked together; and fear follows hope." Spinoza said: "There is no hope without fear, nor fear without hope." And Milton put it, in *Paradise Regained*: "For where no hope is left, is left no fear." Seeking fruition gives hostage to fortune. There can be dangers, and there can be anxiety consequent to dangers only when there are cherished things and resolutions which might be threatened. The overly anxious individual may so crave respite from his fear that he will give up hope in a plaintive bid for inner peace.

Creative effort which taps and explores positive, untried pathways deep within our being arouses disturbing anxiety: for it is an investment in the *future;* and where there is uncertainty of return, one is loath to invest. One knows the *present* state of things to be at least bearable; where confidence in one's capabilities, or in the responsiveness of others, is deficient, such investment in the future is deeply disquieting.

The time lag between present effort and future reward —the suspense which adds spice to the creative efforts of the self-confident—severely depresses those whose anticipation of success is slight. They experience lethargy when they sit down to study or to work at something requiring protracted effort. One well-endowed but ineffectual man described his inability to function on a day he had set aside for a necessary creative task: "I just felt tired. . . . I did not *want* to do it. . . . It did not seem rewarding enough. It seemed like a *waste!*" Not only is *time* thus "wasted," in the conceptions of the anxious, but also self-respect, sense of personal worth. For when the one who is uncertain of the future attempts to create, his anxiety often drives him into some non-creative mode of tension reduction; this non-creative release provides still another instance of failure, or insult to self-concept. The very attempt at creative effort therefore comes to mean danger to the essential sense of personal significance. It is understandable, therefore, that such a man is prone to abandoning a project at the very first sign of difficulty: that is, before he has fully committed himself to the completion of the task, before he has fully staked his self-esteem upon the outcome.

Reasonable predictability of the future is essential to adequate freedom to achieve the constructive possibilities of selfhood. That is why the parent who characteristically breaks promises undercuts the developing child's potential for creative effort. There is an *expectancy* factor. The child or adult who is reasonably confident of eventually receiving mediating rewards can apply himself efficiently over a considerable period of time; but one who is not finds himself beset by intense anxiety which clamors for immediate relief; and the capacity to plan and execute the exploration of self's creative possibilities falls victim to more rapid mechanisms for—temporarily—achieving inner peace. Therefore, there is a need to keep one hand on the "lifesaver" of self-defeatism, else the person feels dread of sinking in a sea of despair. He inwardly senses that if he enters full-heartedly into life's pursuits, and permits himself to be conscientiously constructive, then terrible anxiety, self-depletion, and devastation will ensue. An artisan whose workshop was always a scene of confusion and disorganization attempted to put his tools and materials in order one day and promptly experienced marked depression. "In being methodical I would be *too* constructive," he said.

An individual with such a need continually reassures

himself that he is not "putting all his eggs in one basket," that he does not hope to find peace of mind solely through constructive effort. Such people will sometimes, during psychotherapeutic sessions, employ little gestures which apparently possess no intrinsic purpose, such as examining a ring on the finger, picking at some spot on the hand, scratching oneself unnecessarily, and so on. An essential meaning of these gestures is this: "See here! Don't think that *I* shall abandon myself to working on myself, exploring myself, free associating. I shall rather examine the ring on my finger (which I have had for half my lifetime), pick at a callous (which does not really bother me), and scratch myself as if I were alone. Let these be tokens of my reserve —of my resolve that I shall *not* entirely commit my heart and my hope to creative effort."

Success assists success. A mechanism which has been helpful for anxiety reduction in the past is more likely to be employed again in the future; and the creative exploration of the inner world is such a mechanism. To descend to one's own inner heart, to listen there for faint traces of understandings which are cloaked in primitive symbols, to evaluate these in the light of reason, and to select for execution those which give promise of utility; these too constitute a mechanism bearing upon anxiety reduction. And it is a mechanism, we may add, which bears weightily upon the realization of self's potentials. But this creative approach to the problems of life is a luxury some people cannot afford. For we have seen that creativity involves hope, and that hope opens the door to anxiety.

To embark upon the uncharted seas of selfhood, to reach out creatively to the potentials of life, and to select of these as our own reason permits requires that one be able to bear the anxieties intrinsic to a creative approach; but the one with a gnawing sense of insignificance cannot bear these anxieties adequately. Relatively minor setbacks are for him disasters. Therefore, we find that a creative approach to life—be it in the arts, sciences, or any other life context—can truly evolve only when there is sufficient esteem for the self. For underlying feelings of insignificance draw upon the energies and possibilities of selfhood, and harness these to the pressing purpose of defense against overwhelming mental pain; and these hastily conceived and compulsively executed defenses are likely to bolster self-esteem only temporarily, and to contribute—in a more decisive way—toward lasting self-defeat.

X

REPEATING PATTERNS THAT FAIL

Common sense holds that every human being seeks to succeed in life. Freud's "pleasure principle" and time-tested hedonistic philosophies hold that each will guide himself toward gratification; and human "free will," we tend to believe, will support creative intelligence in this direction.

Strange, therefore, are the phenomena we are about to discuss. Clinical and extra-clinical examples abound in which the individual consistently and persistently follows a course of action which leads not to his long term pleasure, but to pain; not to his success and self-realization, but to repeated self-abuse and resounding failure. Moreover, the pattern is predictable. It tends to be excited by certain precipitating factors; it tends to be acted out through patterns of behavior characterizing that particular individual; it is not sporadic, but rather continual; it is self-defeating, yet self-perpetuating. Why should non-integrative behavior whose self-defeating consequences stand in stark contradiction to man's rational nature persist? Both clinical and everyday observation show that people may persist for years in behavior which repeatedly goes counter to their best interests, and which brings grief to their long term satisfactions. Briefly—why do we repeat patterns that fail? Why do some of us persist in making the same sort of mistakes over and over again? Does not ordinary experience indicate that any thinking organism will look ahead to the consequences of its actions? If the advantages gained by such actions outweigh the unfavorable consequences, that line of behavior will tend to be continued; and if the reverse is true, it will be discontinued. Why then do some of us time and again repeat the very same thing that memory could tell us failed the last time?

Freud sought to explain this unreasonable persistence through assuming an "instinct" to recreate an earlier state of things. According to this view, the individual's contrary behavior to his apparent interests, his violation of Freud's "pleasure principle," his performance of that which brings pain rather than pleasure, his demonstration of no less than a "demonic character" in this regard—all follow from this instinct to recreate a given state. Freud termed this "instinct" the "repetition compulsion," for such people seemed to be in the grip of a compulsion to repeat certain patterns of behavior. And this "repetition compulsion" concept is obviously an excellent description of a puzzling phenomenon, but it still leaves us groping for an explanation and an answer to the question of *why* such behavior persists.

Modern psychologists, armed with laboratory-derived findings, have greatly added to Freud's early insights. In experiments, they have actually succeeded in making animals self-defeating; and they have also "cured" such animals of these self-defeating tendencies. Let us analyze and discuss why we repeat patterns that fail, in the light of these findings. We shall see that certain qualities of human life, under certain conditions, drive us toward these "losing" ways. We shall not only analyze what makes laboratory animals—rats—self-defeating, but we shall also draw direct comparisons to human self-defeating behavior.

One of the factors which pressures us toward repeating patterns that fail is anxiety, in a strictly mechanistic sense. We have already seen (in Chapter 4) how one may defeat himself in order to feel "secure" in the "affection" of others, such as parents. But now we must consider anxiety in a more general sense.

There are ways of binding anxiety other than through the esteem we find in the eyes of people. In adolescence, running to a gymnasium to build muscles is one such activity. In later years, running to the bank to build up an account is analogous. Such activities are anxiety reducers, though not necessarily related to the esteem of others. We are driven from within to such anxiety-reducing activities, for anxiety has *drive* properties: it impels us to do something in order to keep its level down to certain limits. We saw, in Chapter 4, how imperative are the pressures exerted by anxiety.

First: Any reaction pattern that actually serves to reduce anxiety is a "rewarding" pattern as far as a person's emotional needs are concerned.

Second: We know, in line with basic learning theory, that any such "rewarding" pattern of response becomes "stamped in," and therefore persists. This agrees with common sense: We tend to repeat behavior that permits us to lower anxiety.

Third: A pattern of response may serve admirably to lower anxiety, but fail dismally regarding success in life. Obvious examples here are chronic alcoholism, drug addiction, and avoidance of work.

Fourth: When a pattern of response serves to reduce anxiety, then, in time, we crave to repeat that pattern.

Fifth: If this anxiety-reducing behavior happens to be self-defeating in regard to the individual's long term goals, this is unfortunate; but it does not at all preclude the repeated use of this self-defeating pattern in the individual's daily efforts toward maintaining freedom from anxiety.

Sixth: We know that various reaction patterns become fixed according to the degree to which they permit drive reduction—in this instance, anxiety reduction. Therefore, it follows that such self-defeating patterns are reinforced by the anxiety reduction which attends their use, and that such patterns tend to be self-perpetuating.

The circle is now complete. On a mechanistic level, we now know one reason why we repeat patterns that fail: to reduce anxiety.

Another way to say it is this: Behavior may be *adjustive* without being *adaptive*. That is, behavior may permit anxiety reduction without in the least assisting the individual's long term welfare. It may even be seriously injurious to it.

The psychologist Judson S. Brown, as reported by O. Hobart Mowrer,[1] provided an ingenious experiment in which rats were made into self-defeatists. Let us follow it closely, for it helps us to understand our own self-defeatism.

In this experiment a rat is put at one end of an alley several feet long; if, after a period of ten seconds, the floor of the alley—consisting of a metal grill—is electrified, the rat will run to the opposite end of the alley and escape into a nonelectrified compartment, thereby escaping the mild electric shock.

After some repetition, the rat will run this course as soon as he is placed upon the grill, even before any shock is administered. This makes sense, since the rat has learned that in this place, in the past, he received a mildly painful shock. When he perceives the danger situation, that is, when he sees the alley with its grill, he becomes frightened;

since running into the end compartment proved in the past to be a successful way to avoid pain and reduce fear, he will therefore start to run even when the electricity has not yet been turned on, and the grill is shock free.

So far there is no self-defeat. The animal is behaving in an intelligent way. He tends to avoid the metal grill that he associates with past pain and fear. Moreover, when the shocks are delayed more than ten seconds, he continues to behave intelligently: He runs at a more leisurely pace. Should the shocks be discontinued completely, in time the animal will make an intelligent adaptation, and cease running altogether.

Thus far the phenomena fit exactly what we know about learning and conditioning. An animal learns an avoidance reaction in response to fear; this avoidance reaction (running) is gradually subject to extinction if fear is no longer excited by the situation.

But here is the surprising part. If after the running response has been established, the right half of the floor grill—at the far end of the alley—is permanently electrified so that in making his run the rat always receives a brief shock just before arriving at the safety compartment, the running response is *not* extinguished. In other words, even though the rat never receives another shock in the left half of the alley, where he is introduced, and even though he need only sit still, or limit his wandering to the left half of the alley to avoid shock indefinitely, yet he will consistently run toward and over the right half of the grill, thus receiving electric shocks before escaping to the safety compartment.

This surely is self-defeating behavior! The animals certainly seem to manifest a "need for punishment," a "masochistic trend." How can we explain this self-defeating behavior? How can we explain this consistent repetition of a pattern which brings unnecessary pain? We surely want to explain it, for the similarity to our own self-defeating patterns must be obvious. How many of us return time and again to situations that hurt us far more than their temporary "benefits"? What makes us return repeatedly to such situations?

In a brilliant analysis (that goes considerably beyond our level) Mowrer offers an explanation, which we summarize in our version as follows: We must bear in mind two sorts of factors: 1) What is it that *arouses* anxiety? and 2) How is the anxiety *reduced*?

As to the first: The very sight of that part of the alley where the rat is introduced is for the rat a cause for feeling anxiety (or, if you will, "fear," which we use interchangeably in our discussion). For this sight is associated with painful electric shock in the rat's past experience, and therefore becomes a "conditioned stimulus" for the arousal of anxiety.

We humans also learn to be frightened—rendered severely anxious—by various situations. Going to work, speaking to the boss, starting to do anything really constructive, giving wholehearted effort to a project, getting near the one we love: these, and many more situations we have already discussed, can be "conditioned stimuli" that can render each of us severely anxious.

As to the second: How the anxiety is reduced is rather clear in the case of the rat. It is simply that he *runs*. In the past he had found such running to be, eventually, successful in achieving a reduction of anxiety.

We humans do somewhat more complex things, but for the same reason. We do things that afford us anxiety reduction. If one avoids going to work, if one thwarts and subtly irritates the boss, if one wastes one's time, if one never really gives full effort to anything, if one goads one's sweetheart or mate into a reluctant fury: all these things afford, in devious ways, the reduction of a drive such as anxiety.

In the case of the rat, the arousal and reduction of anxiety form a complete and self-sustaining cycle. It is complete because it involves a tension increase—anxiety due to seeing the alley—and a tension decrease—the lowering of anxiety through running. It is self-sustaining because the running response becomes more and more "stamped in" and reinforced due to its being "successful" in eventually achieving the anxiety reduction afforded by the safety compartment. But the rat did not really have to run at all, in order to avoid being shocked. All he had to do was sit still, or limit his wandering to the left half of the alley. Yet he repeatedly chose a course of action which brought him pain, which defeated him in his efforts to avoid being shocked, but which *did* afford a temporary reduction in anxiety.

In much the same way, humans repeat patterns by which they defeat themselves, yet bring about anxiety reduction. And these self-defeating patterns are also self-sustaining, thus creating a "vicious circle" of self-defeatism. A protective device may relieve anxiety for the moment, but eventually lead to the creation of new (and more severe) anxiety. For example, a man may remain in an unsatisfying job situation so as to avoid the anxiety and guilt which attend spontaneous seeking after self-realization; but after some years of being bogged down in this unsatisfactory work, deep anxieties, related to his need for self-fulfillment, may emerge and play havoc with his mental health. Yet these emerging anxieties may make him cling to what he "has" even more rigidly: *ergo* the "vicious circle."

Brown's rats, as Mowrer points out, exemplify an experimental analogue of this "vicious circle" of self-defeatism. The rats become anxious upon seeing the apparatus and run as a device to reduce anxiety; but such running causes them to receive further shock (which could have been avoided by not running at all); this further shock conditions more strongly the fear of the apparatus, and each "success" in reaching the "safety compartment" reinforces more strongly the self-defeating mechanism of running as an anxiety-reducing device. Thus we can understand why—as Horney had developed earlier in the clinical setting—a "vicious circle" attends the neurotic paradox: Behavior that is self-defeating may be self-perpetuating.

Now, one might ask: "Why did not the rats learn that running was self-defeating? After all, in the end phase of the experiment they were not shocked until they stepped on the *electrified* half of the grill. Why did not they learn, in time, simply not to run that far?" These are excellent questions, which have direct bearing on how humans correct patterns of self-defeat. To answer these questions, U. E. Whiteis performed a follow-up experiment which was reported by Mowrer [2] as an addendum to his original paper.

Whiteis' experiment appears to have been essentially the same as Brown's except for this important feature: Whiteis made the right (shock) half of the alley a different color and pattern from that of the left, so that, through this and other cues, the rat could readily distinguish between the two halves. Now, note this critically important finding: *Once the animal could discriminate between these two—between the shock-producing half and the non-shock half—the self-defeating flight into punishment ceased!*

The implications of these findings are tremendously important. They offer experimental validation of ancient wisdom—to the effect that "truth," "knowledge," "insight"

—whatever you wish to call it—that *knowing* is helpful in life, that knowing about one's life space and its forces helps one dissolve self-defeating ways, and find a more satisfactory existence.

We shall have more to say about this in our chapter on psychotherapy. But here, we underline the fact that when the rat can better "know" the circumstances under which he defeats himself, when he can better identify that portion of the grill where he receives electric shock, then he is better able to avoid repeating a "failing" pattern.

In the same way, when we humans are made aware of our self-defeating habits, we too can better dissolve them. This self-awareness is critical to constructive self-guidance and self-correction. For self-defeating habits may arise without our being aware of them and may continue to operate for long periods of time, again without benefit of consciousness. This lack of adequate awareness makes for their perpetuation and their continuing operation in our lives. The learning of habits depends more upon how "useful" these habits are for bringing about tension reduction than it does upon conscious understanding; therefore a self-defeating way of responding to people and to life may come into being, and be repeatedly reinforced without insight into what is actually taking place. Since such dissociated self-defeating ways of behaving exist and operate outside awareness, they are not perceived by the individual himself. They continue to operate without the self-appraisal, self-evaluation, and self-criticism so essential to optimal growth. And since they thus escape rational self-criticism, they may exist indefinitely as essentially blind modes of achieving anxiety reduction.

Another reason for our repetition of "losing" patterns is this: An act may have more than a single consequence; that is, it is often rewarding in some respects and punishing in others. And we showed that the *time* element may be very different indeed regarding these part motives. Specifically, an act may serve admirably for the *immediate* reduction of a drive, but very poorly in terms of *later* needs such as long term interests.

For example, Brown's rat that started to run as soon as he saw the grill relieved his momentary anxiety, but paid for such relief shortly thereafter in the form of electric shock. Similarly, the chronic alcoholic who enters a bar instead of seeking employment relieves his immediate anxiety with a series of acts which bode ill for *future* anxiety status. Thus, a self-defeating pattern may be harmful to one aspect of personality, but deeply gratifying to another. And the gratification may be far swifter than the hurt.

Mowrer and Ullman[3] have demonstrated experimentally that the longer the "hurt" is delayed, the more self-defeating and "foolish" are rats likely to be in their behavior. That is, when the rat has a choice in his conduct, he is likely to be "wiser" in choosing the best path for himself if the punishment for a poor choice is administered quickly.

This time factor surely enters into an explanation of our own foolishness, too. We humans possess vastly greater reasoning powers than the rat: Our capacity for employing symbols—to bring the past and the probable future into the psychological present—is prodigious indeed. Yet we all have limitations; and some of our rigidity in repeating patterns that fail—patterns which are more punishing than rewarding—is due to such a time factor: witness the eating of green fruit by youngsters, and overextended installment buying by their elders. Indeed, some of the punishing consequences of self-defeating behavior enormously dwarf the immediate rewards. But these punishing features make their appearance so very long after the act which brings immediate reward that this time factor causes the slight immediate reward to outweight the greater but more remote punishment, and works toward our repeating and perpetuating the self-defeating habit pattern. This is the issue of *partially* adequate behavior as against *integrative* response. The former deals with immediate tensions, but does not sufficiently take into account the time factor—the future tensions and their optimal gratification and relief.

To restate: Self-defeat is drive reducing, but does not balance consequences more remote in time; it is deficient in scope of adjustment; it overemphasizes the immediate tensions of anxiety and guilt at the expense of less pressing but no less important needs for self-esteem and self-realization; it reduces anxiety in an immediate sense, but has the delayed effect of increasing it.

Coming late for appointments, keeping friends and business associates waiting, failure to complete one's assignments, repeated loss of one's position—all these serve to bring about the tension reduction we have described. But the individual persists in reacting to the present, as if the conditions of childhood still prevailed; and he does not sufficiently employ the symbolic processes of speech and thinking, which bring into the present more remote goals and desiderata.

Self-defeat, then, is overly bound to the present in terms of pressure toward drive reduction; to the past in terms of retention of established patterns formerly proven effective for such drive reduction; and is not sufficiently linked to the future and its long term implications. This imbalance contributes to the "vicious circle" of self-defeatism. Such behavior, momentarily employed for immediate gain, for release of tension, may have remote consequences which worsen the individual's life situation and render his chances of bettering it slender. Thus, the emotionally maladjusted may walk a treadmill of self-defeat, which energizes and perpetuates itself: The individual walks the treadmill to relieve his anxiety, and the longer he stays on it, the more deeply established becomes his *need* to stay on it.

The very *intensity* of the anxiety is a factor which works toward repeating patterns that fail. This was cleverly demonstrated in an experiment by the psychologist I. E. Farber.[4] Farber trained two groups of rats to run a T-maze, in search of food. (The T-maze is simply a small maze in the form of a "T".) The T-maze is useful, for when the rat comes to the end of the stem of the maze he has a clear choice as to whether to turn into the right or the left part of the bar of the T. The rat is motivated to make this choice, since food—his reward—is placed at one end of this upper bar.

Farber divided the rats into two groups. One group, the "control group," simply ran one hundred trials, receiving food with each successfully completed run. The other group of rats, the "experimental group," was given forty trials which were identical with those of the control group; but during the last sixty trials of the learning series, the experimental group was given an electric shock. This electric shock was administered immediately after the rat made the choice as to which way to run.

After completion of the trials, Farber did two things: 1) He shifted the food to the opposite side of the maze, and 2) he ceased all electric shocks. The rats were now permitted to run the maze in search of food and Farber kept track of the number of trials that were required for each rat to learn that the food had been switched, and also to change his habitual way of turning so as to deal realistically with these altered conditions.

The question was: Which group of rats would learn to

change more quickly—those which had been shocked during the last sixty runs, or those which had been shock-free?

The results were dramatically clear-cut. The shocked animals required *many* more trials to change their ways properly than did the unshocked rats; the mean runs required for such learning being 61.12 for the shocked rats, whereas only 9.71 runs were required, on the average, for the others; and this difference was unquestionably significant statistically—that is, it was a difference which could not at all be reasonably accounted for by chance.

Some of us may not relish the analogy, but Farber had in fact created a situation similar to human self-defeat. Each animal had an opportunity to choose a path toward being "successful" in finding food for himself (and the timing was such that each was quite sure to be hungry), yet the previously shocked rats were somehow not free to use their intelligence to make the success-linked choice; rather, they persisted in a self-initiated path which led to failure and continued hunger. These "self-defeating" animals were just as intelligent as the "control" group, for they were just as successful during the forty trials which preceded the application of electric shock.

How can we explain such behavior? Why should the shocked rats persist more than the unshocked rats in making choices which were self-defeating? The answer appears to be that while both groups of rats were under the drive pressure of hunger—sufficient to motivate them toward exploration and learning—they were different in one important respect: *the degree of anxiety experienced.*

We may assume that the unshocked rats suffered some degree of anxiety, too. After all, they did have to run a maze in search of food, and success was not assured; past experience had taught them that many efforts would end in a "blind alley." But the *degree* of anxiety experienced by these unshocked rats must surely have been less than that suffered by their shocked brothers, who not only had to "worry" about whether or not they would find food, but also about the frightening shock which they associated with the sight of the critical juncture in the maze.

We know what strong anxiety does to us. It causes us to "freeze"; it makes us rigid. That is the answer as to why the shocked rats persisted in repeating patterns that failed. The extra anxiety made for rigidity, for a lesser freedom to evaluate the new situation and to choose the wiser path. It made instead for a self-defeating repetition of the established mode of anxiety reduction, *ergo* their extremely poor showing in learning the new path to the food long after the shocks had ceased to exist.

We may note how closely Farber's experimental conditions, as we interpret them, resemble those of human life. If we select two groups of children, those with loving parents and those with essentially rejecting and competitive ones, we have analogues of Farber's subjects. For the loved (and therefore emotionally secure) children will go through their developmental years under the pressures of hunger, self-realization, desire for companionship, sex, and so on; the unloved children will have, in addition to these pressures, the added anxiety of anticipating severe rejection concerning things which are beyond their control. This parental rejection and its attending severe anxiety are surely analogous to the electric shock which had been applied to Farber's rats at the T-maze juncture.

When the "secure" children approach life's choices, they are under pressure to realize themselves, and, as in the instance of Farber's unshocked rats, this intrinsic pressure assists learning and development. Encouraged by the parent who is permissive and genuinely warm, the child is free to think and explore his repertoire of responses for the "best" that is within himself. But the insecure children, those who have met rejection (shock) without really knowing why, approach life's very same choices and challenges with added anxiety, since they are at a loss to understand these "shocks" of parental rejection.

The cues which set off anxiety, for the rats, were associated with the T-juncture of the maze. Analogously, anxiety invoking cues for the children may be associated with any contact with significant persons; and also with any choice bearing upon self-realization, on the one hand, or essential immaturity, on the other.

Farber's formerly shocked rats "handled" their anxiety by compulsively taking a fixed turn in the maze. The taking of this turn had proven itself to be an immediately functioning anxiety-reducing device; but when conditions were altered, so that a different turn was required for success, the continued adherence to the old response was self-defeating.

Analogously, insecure children, repeatedly shocked by parental rejection, also learn devices which relieve immediate anxiety. When conditions are altered, and the children attempt to adjust to the world outside the home, they, too, cling to their old anxiety-reducing devices and in such rigid adherence to immature patterns resides the formula for lifelong self-defeat. The pity of it is that just as Farber's rats persevered in making the fixed response long after all shock had ceased, so do these children (and subsequent adults) continue to respond to people—even those quite willing to accept them—*as if the rejection of childhood is still to be met.*

Such strong anxiety, with its attendant rigidity, plays havoc with the developing child's, and the later adult's general unfolding of self's possibilities. But it is especially devastating in the unfolding of their creativity, for creating involves ambiguity. It involves the ability to think conditionally, to pursue a line of thought or action *as if* certain things were true; yet the creator is not sure of whether these things are actually true, or ever will be.

The strongly anxious individual is less able to tolerate the abstract or ambiguous. He wants to *know* and to know definitely; for he is perplexed by too many unanswered questions emanating from the world within. He desires concreteness in the world without, to compensate for the inner indefiniteness, and to overbalance the ill-structured feelings which beset him—feelings which are severely disquieting, yet have no adequate identifiable cause.

There is also a time element in creating. One cannot "force" a new idea or a novel approach to emerge. It must emerge from within ourselves, and it characteristically requires an unpredictable and often considerable amount of time for this emergence. Therefore, during this period of ambiguity, the strongly anxious individual is liable to abort the creative process and to seek a more immediate solution for his disquiet. The time element and its attending pain predispose the individual to less than adequate modes of finding relief, to short cuts which widen the gap between creative potential and actual accomplishment. The flexibility of man, the ability to change one's "set" with ease, the inner freedom to offer hypotheses—to step out of the conventional path into new regions of thought —are essential to creativity. The distinguished American psychologist Carl Rogers phrased it this way: "It is from this spontaneous toying and exploration that there arises the hunch, the creative seeing of life in a new and significant way."

But severe anxiety makes for rigidity of thought. It is

behind the "resistance" encountered in psychotherapy, where the patient employs all sorts of techniques to prevent knowledge of his inner self, to preserve the rigid *status quo* in his thought processes. Anxiety furnishes the force which resists insight; and such resistance to possibilities which emerge from within the self curtail and limit the dimensions of evolving selfhood. It tends toward unwieldy repetitiveness, toward an irrational clinging to unsuccessful approaches in the solution of life problems, toward rigidity in personality, and toward the compulsive renunciation of that freedom of movement intrinsic to creative intelligence. It lends itself to the establishment of a "vicious circle" in one's approach to life in which anxiety lends itself to failure, and failure leads to further anxiety, reinforcing the rigidity of the prevailing attitudes and point of view. The anticipation of failure, for example, caused one man to rush headlong into every new project, for the waiting intrinsic to methodical approach was more than he could bear; such anxiety-linked inadequacies in planning and attention to details worked increasingly toward further failure.

Strong protracted anxiety is conducive to only a *pseudo*-freedom for creative achievement, for such apparent creativity as takes place under such conditions serves escape *from* the unbearable, rather than approach *toward* the truly and positively desired. There is a defensive compulsiveness to such escape behavior which lacks the spontaneity and quiet expansive gratification of naturally unfolding self-expression.

Escape from such anxiety may virtually constitute a way of life. When anxiety is sufficiently severe and prolonged, one may relinquish the positive urges of life, and seek only relief and secure protection against recurrences. This is especially true when humiliation—insult to self-concept

—attended prior periods of anxiety, as in instances of early poverty. Such people may, for example, devote the rest of their lives to accumulating money in order to be "secure" from further anxiety-laden humiliation.

One sorry outcome of this orientation to life is that the individual sometimes ceases to know what he is working *for*. Since he has worked so long *against* feeling anxious, the positive joys and unfolding of selfhood no longer enter into his life space, he no longer knows what to go *toward*. This situation illustrates the principle that a mode of reaction which initially develops as a defense may become a cul-de-sac in which is lost the positive unfolding of life's possibilities. Thus, "repeating patterns that fail" may become a basic blueprint for the conduct of one's life. For in truth these patterns do indeed "succeed" in terms of immediate tension reduction, but fail dismally regarding life's vital developmental tasks and central issues of self-realization.

Such self-defeating behavior, whether it be slight or great in its effect, serves to bleed off anxiety and to support the immediate need for tension reduction. But it does not deal remedially with problems, and is therefore both self-perpetuating and self-destructive. It is self-perpetuating because it permits immediate anxiety reduction, and is therefore further "stamped in" on the basis of the reinforcement of drive-reducing patterns of response. It is self-defeating, not only in its specific form (digging pits to later fall into) but also in its general nature. That is, the immediate dissipation of anxiety, without remedying the fundamental causes, is a waste of time and energy; and such wastes can, in the long run, produce serious impoverishment of the personality.

Therefore, the task of the individual who seeks self-realization must include the detection of such enervating modes of meeting one's daily anxiety, and the gradual substitution of constructive defenses for those which are sub-optimal and unproductive. For the hardening of these non-creative modes of anxiety reduction into habit, and the sinking of these habits into the realm of the unconscious, drain one's being of the promise inherent in creative intelligence, and render the self ill equipped for the optimal realization of its human potentials.

NOTES

[1] O. Hobart Mowrer, *Learning Theory and Personality Dynamics* (New York: The Ronald Press Company, 1950), pp. 258–260 and 510–513. The field of psychology is indebted to Dr. Mowrer for basic contributions, and I am personally indebted to him for some of the ideas contained in this chapter.

[2] *Ibid.*, pp. 260–261.

[3] O. Hobart Mowrer and Albert D. Ullman, "Time as a Determinant in Integrative Learning" in *Psychological Review*, Vol. 52 (1945), pp. 61–90, reprinted in Mowrer, *op. cit.*, pp. 418–454.

[4] I. E. Farber, "Response Fixation Under Anxiety and Non-Anxiety Conditions" in *Journal of Experimental Psychology*, Vol. 38 (1948), pp. 111–131.

XI

PSYCHOTHERAPY AND PATTERNS
OF SELF-DEFEAT[1]

We turn now to consider the use of psychotherapy in assisting the individual to achieve a fuller measure of self-realization, to concrete therapeutic procedures, and to their underlying meanings. We shall pay particular attention to the dissolution of self-defeating patterns in life. And we shall relate certain techniques of therapy to the freeing of creative potentials.

First, let us note an immediate difficulty we encounter: It is extremely difficult to perceive and to see clearly the actual meanings of self-and-other defeat in life; for human destructiveness is shocking. To conceive of people capable of harming themselves and others *as a way of life* is frankly painful and frightening. We therefore tend to dissociate it—to thrust it beyond the fringes of awareness —in our conception of man's ways. It is far more pleasant and reassuring to believe that people are consistently constructive in what they "intend" to do. Moreover, we all rationalize our failures well, so there is no dearth of "good," sufficient, and quite respectable reasons for consistently falling short of one's potential. Further, our culture trains us early in the skills of dissimulation, so that our hostilities find ready camouflaged outlets.

All these things weigh against our truly seeing the self-defeat in our daily operations. These, and other resistance factors that we shall consider as we progress, tend to maintain the façade by which we explain to ourselves and to others the reasons we fall short of what we know we can do and accomplish in life.

In the psychotherapeutic setting, however, these camouflages often prove transparent; for the therapeutic situation is a peculiarly structured one, in which the patient is expected to behave in a manner considerably different from his customary one but with which the therapist is quite thoroughly familiar, since he ordinarily possesses considerable experience with a wide variety of persons in this particular setting. The self-defeating patient, therefore, finds himself out of his medium, whereas the fully trained therapist is very much at home. The result is often that the patient's skills at rationalization and dissimulation are pierced, and his lifelong self-defeating patterns come nakedly to the fore.

PROCESSES OF PSYCHOTHERAPY

The patient's task in psychotherapy is simply this: *to say what comes to mind, as it comes to mind.* This is Freud's "fundamental rule" of analysis. It involves gradual self-sensitivization to noticing inner phenomena—the increases and decreases of tension, the feelings and peripheral ideation—the things generally overlooked in life.

This seemingly easy task is actually far from simple.

It is complicated by those many qualities which accompany self-defeatism. The individual whose creativity is stifled, for example, cannot permit himself to drift along in "free" associating. He craves power; the powerful person *directs* his thinking; the patient therefore does likewise to an untoward extent, and thereby continually violates Freud's fundamental rule. He is also overly sensitive to slurs against his glorified image of self; revelations frequently imply such slurs, so he therefore tends to maintain inhibitions to self-knowledge, thereby retarding the analysis.

In general, the processes of psychotherapy center around increasing one's awareness of emotional attitudes and feelings. A fundamental premise is this: If a need is known to consciousness, the individual can, in the long run, make a more wholesome and integrated adjustment to life than if the need exists in the unconscious alone. Analogously, if one is *aware* that a nail protrudes from a shoe and is damaging the flesh, one is more likely to have it removed.

Therefore, the therapist encourages free expression. For through such expression are bared not only emotional needs, but also emotional attitudes which block expression (and, in the extra-clinical life, which block self-realization). Observing the "fundamental rule"—seeking to report what comes to mind as it comes to mind—offers a sensitive and comprehensive approach to both underlying emotional needs and emotional blocks. Awareness is thus extended. Self-discovery is fostered. The processes of truth play about emotional attitudes and inner feelings. Such usage of awareness permits a self-educative interaction. Feelings gradually broaden and modify understanding; reason gently molds feelings, rendering them more valid in the light of reality.

In the preceding chapter, we saw how critically important it was for rats to "know" the circumstances of their life-situations if they were to avoid self-defeat. By way of reminder, let us recall that Brown's rats were compulsively self-defeating, that they ran headlong onto the electrified half of a grill, and subjected themselves to extremely unpleasant experiences, when all they had to do to avoid the unpleasantness was simply either to run elsewhere, or to sit still. We recall that Whiteis' rats, which were essentially identical with Brown's, continued the self-defeatism *until one thing was done.* That thing was this: Help was given to the rats, in the form of inserting a distinctive color and pattern into one half of the alley, thus enabling the animals to make a sharper discrimination between that half of the floor which was shock-inducing, and that half which was shock free. When the animals could clearly distinguish between the dangerous portion of the grid and the half which posed no danger, they ceased to manifest the self-defeating behavior.

Psychotherapy similarly helps the human to distinguish between real dangers in one's present world and those which possessed danger long ago, or which never truly possessed substantial danger, but were only believed to possess it because of immature perceptual apparatus insufficient for the task of adequate recognition. Therapeutic techniques are complex, but permit this generalization: They are aimed at assisting the self-defeatist to separate accurately the realistic grounds for fear and anxiety from those not warranting such emotional valence. Again, when we, as Whiteis' rats, can better distinguish between true dangers and fancied ones, our patterns of adaptation become markedly more realistic and materially less self-defeating. This follows the sequence often evidenced in clinical practice: that a maladaptive habit is more readily changed when the anxiety underlying that habit is first subjected to change.

Thus, insights are sought and achieved in therapy. In the rapport between therapist and patient, self-expression and its attendant recognition and clarification of inner feelings and understandings enable the patient to become more aware of motives and essential factors in his life space. He can increasingly see and choose voluntarily, in areas of his life formerly beyond perception and therefore governed involuntarily. Understandings descend deeper as therapy progresses. The "problem" identified by the patient as the reason for entering treatment often does not turn out to be the *essential* problem in his life, but only a temporary focus of his anxiety.

One man, for example, who entered treatment because of sexual difficulties, found that the more essential problem was in *relating* to other humans, rather than in sex per se. He discovered: "I am aware now of the power struggle on all sides—with my wife, with my boss—even with my little son." Accordingly, though our discussions dealt mainly with other facets of interpersonal relations, in time his sexual difficulties disappeared.

Group therapy is often particularly helpful, for it is often easier to see something in another, and through interaction "one hand washes the other," so to speak. This was made clear in an individual session (that followed such a group experience) with a man who had for years rigidly defended himself against self-knowledge: "I can see how Mary and Dave (group members) defeat themselves—but I have trouble seeing it in myself. . . . But Mary pointed out my own self-defeatism, the other night."

Therapy is not an intellectual process alone: It also embraces emotional experience, for the personality came into being through emotional experiences, which involved glandular and other soma-related reactions and residuals. For therapy to produce truly deep personality changes, it must again involve such intense, repeated, and protracted emotional experiences that the emotional aspects of personality may again be involved and undergo change. Otherwise, as may occur with inexperienced or ill-trained therapists, analysis is a series of academic discussions which yield a superficial grasp of technical jargon and psycho-analytic theory but little or no personality change.

Care is ordinarily taken to avoid advice giving. The patient must assume responsibility for his own behavior, for deciding upon a course of action which, until therapists somehow learn to be omniscient and omnipotent, is only reasonable.

Interpretations are made by the therapist from time to time. But care is taken to provide little more than a nudge in order to avoid the impression that the therapist will do the patient's thinking for him. The goal of therapy is not a parcel of advice, but the resolution of inner conflict, the freeing of the creative intelligence for lifelong self-guidance, and self-advice.

Observing the "fundamental rule"—saying what comes to mind as it comes to mind—is an exercise in creative effort. For it aims at producing, at bringing forth associations, thoughts, and feelings, as part of a constructive project. In this process, attitudes regarding creativity which took shape during childhood are re-enacted in the present. These attitudes are displayed in the relationship with the therapist (the so-called "transference"), in the content of the not-so-free associations, and in the many dimensions which characterize the flow of these associations: their sequence, direction, timing, dearth or flood, implicit blocks, and so on. The sophisticated therapist will perceive, in this multi-dimensional adult situation, a re-enactment containing all the essential early attitudes toward creative self-fulfillment in life. The patient tends to repeat self-defeating patterns within the therapeutic situation, for the microcosm of the clinic contains all the essential features of the world at large: interpersonal relations, threats to significance, anxiety, and the other dynamics involved in self-defeat. Characteristic behavior patterns for handling such relations, threats, attitudes, and feelings, will tend to be repeated.

First, the patient comes to see *what* he is doing. Next, he learns *why* he does it; i.e., first he comes to perceive his self-defeatism and next, he searches for the motivational meaning behind it.

We analyze the function of such self-defeating behavior in terms of the inner economy. We explore and identify the role of defeatism in binding anxiety and depression, and in buttressing the sense of personal significance, albeit through some measure of self-destruction. Such rising to awareness of long-repressed ideas and feelings is extremely painful. The Freudian concept of "resistance" refers to the forces which prevent such self-knowledge. These forces are very considerable, for we all fear to relinquish operating defenses, however self-defeating. We all fear to relinquish relative security to again face intolerable conflict and uncertainty. In brief, established ways of defending oneself against anxiety are challenged by therapy; such anxiety therefore tends to break into awareness; and such breakthrough tends to prevent further self-exploration.

Resistance thus tends to perpetuate the entrenched self-defeating security operations. We therefore deal with it as soon and as directly as is feasible. We identify the form it takes (such as silences, superficiality, or diversionary hostility), discuss the patient's fear of coming to grips with his problem, and gradually discover the sorts of unconscious elements the revelation of which is so threatening (in our culture usually related to sex or hostility) as to block treatment to such an extent.

At the turn of the century, at the very dawn of psychoanalytic understanding, it was believed that specific "forgotten scenes" of past life were the cause of emotional difficulties. Accordingly, it was believed—as it was by the Viennese neurologist Joseph Breuer, working in collaboration with Sigmund Freud—that adequate therapy consisted of "catharsis." That is, psychotherapy involved simply the uncovering and draining away of such forgotten episodes, the "abreaction" of an event, much as one would find and destroy a specific disease-producing microbe, or as in the primitive practice of bloodletting. This is still the conception of psychotherapy which prevails in current popular drama, for it is a conception which lends itself to sustained interest and dramatic climax.

However, we have since learned the necessary role of repetition, both in the causation and therapy of personality difficulties. We know now that specific isolated events seldom cause crippling emotional difficulties. Rather, adequate causes of neurosis are far more likely to occur thousands of times in the life of the individual, and such repetition is likely to be required over a considerable period of time for personality warping to be effected and to overcome health. Similarly, the processes of psychotherapy seldom involve a single dramatic revelation capable of producing prolonged self-sustaining positive personality change. Instead, adequate treatment usually involves very considerable repetition—both during sessions and between sessions—for the extinction of conditioned learnings, and for the "counterconditioning" of new patterns of response.

Such repetition is analogous to that in conditioning experiments in which Pavlov repeatedly presented food and simultaneously rang a bell, so that his dogs eventually salivated when he rang the bell even when no food was presented. This is comparable to the development of personality maladjustment; that is, it parallels the growth and perpetuation of some sub-optimal response which attends prolonged social experience.

If, for example, a child is made anxious by a derogatory and overcritical parent whenever he seeks to accomplish anything, he comes to associate anxiety with the very act of seeking to achieve, and later in life, continues to experience anxiety in his work and creative life even when no parent is present, and when, realistically, there is no longer an *outer* basis for such anxiety.

Pavlov soon noted that if he repeatedly sounded the bell without presenting any more food, in time, the salivary response would gradually lessen, and finally cease. This is termed "experimental extinction." This sort of extinction of a learned response is parallel to what goes on during therapy. A situation is re-created in which an authority figure (the therapist) is present when the patient airs his hopes for self-realization and achievement; instead of sensing rejection whenever he mentions his realistic hopes for creative success, the patient is repeatedly exposed to genuine, positive, professional interest in his full maturation. The old responses to this situation—anxiety and guilt—are therefore gradually supplanted, and the patient's valid ambitions are gradually associated with real support for his sense of personal worth. The point is that considerable repetition is required, both in laboratory experimental extinction and in clinical psychotherapeutic extinction and counterconditioning of sub-optimal patterns of response.

In this context, we can understand how successful "therapy" has been done with self-defeating rats. We recall that Farber, as described in the preceding chapter, had caused rats to be self-defeating by conditioning them to the experience of strong anxiety. This strong anxiety caused rigidity in their thinking at the very times when it was important for them to be "flexible." Because of this rigidity, they persisted in making the "wrong" choices, thus defeating themselves. Farber reasoned that if the rats' anxiety level could be lowered, they would be less rigid in their thinking, and behave more intelligently. He therefore employed an anxiety-reducing device. His purpose was to *decondition* the rats to anxiety regarding the cues to which they would be exposed in approaching the choice point in the maze. This "therapy" receiving group of rats, by design, would experience considerably less anxiety as they approached the T-juncture than equally self-defeating rats which had been denied such "therapy." His findings were clear and conclusive. Self-defeating rats which received such "therapy" subsequently proved to perform far better than equally self-defeating rats which had not received such "treatment."

Somewhat simplified, let us summarize: Initially, Farber's rats had been shocked at the T-maze choice point. Consequently, the severe anxiety which they experienced upon approaching this choice point made them compulsively self-defeating. But through new experiences at this choice-point—being permitted to feed at that very spot, without unpleasantness—they gradually lost the anxiety associated with that place (anxiety which was now unrealistic, since all electric shock had ceased to be administered). Having been exposed to such counterconditioning, the unrealistic anxiety fell off in intensity, and the rats' adaptive success improved markedly and significantly. Similarly, new experiences with a therapist—a reasonable authority figure—help counteract the frightening experiences previously undergone repeatedly with parents and other significant figures. In this way, the self-defeatist is helped to overcome baseless fears and anxieties (which had previously possessed bases in infancy and childhood), now as grossly unrealistic as the anxiety experienced by Farber's rats.

Unconscious hostility, as we have noted, is frequently a destroyer of the creative approach to life. Our task in therapy therefore involves identification of the forms such hostility takes in thought and expression, discovery of its causes in the world of today and in that of years gone by, and, finally, its direction toward constructive channels. Such identification is not a simple task. The patient has been acting out his self-and-other defeatism for many years. We want him to stop acting out his impulses and feelings in such ways, and to verbalize them instead. This is an extremely painful transition. It is far more comfortable, in an immediate sense, to vent impulses and feelings through minimally considered and overt action than to note carefully and introspectively what is going on.

The "transference" is of invaluable help here. One could talk for years about what takes place outside the clinic without making a real dent in a severe neurosis or character disorder. But when the patient becomes aware of what is actually taking place *right there* in the therapist's office, it has a shockingly vivid and concrete meaning—giving him reason to pause, to reflect, and to perceive himself in a new and more illuminating light. The transference refers to the re-enactment of attitudes and feelings developed in childhood within the patient-therapist relationship. Specifically, we are interested here in the re-creation of intense hatred (and related feelings) toward the therapist, a hatred which has no realistic cause in the present, but rather stems from old wounds. It requires considerable training and professional dedication even to begin to deal adequately with such unconscious hostility, for we all enjoy a pleasant relationship. For quite a while, an optimal therapeutic relationship is very far indeed from being pleasant.

Optimally, the therapist permits the self-defeatist's characteristic modes of behavior to find sufficient expression in the therapeutic relationship; he carefully collects sufficient evidence of hatred in the patient's modes of dealing with life, and only after careful organization of this evidence does he confront the patient with its manifest patterns. To prematurely interpret such hostility and its consequent self-defeatism, and to discuss these things without clear and convincing evidence, would be simply to fail in reaching the patient's understanding. He would deny the validity of the interpretation and continue to dissociate his self-defeatism and its associated hatred; he would gather his defenses even more rigidly about himself.

This is where the phenomena of transference, the actual interaction within the clinic walls, are of service. For these are quite recognizable occurrences, which may be examined immediately and concretely, and are therefore relatively difficult to deny. Yet even these signs of unconscious hatred may be difficult to gather, for the self-defeatist is a deeply frightened person who has long practiced the disguise of his resentment. It may finally fall to a relatively small element to be the wedge whereby an opening is made through which the inner seething caldron of hatred may finally be viewed.

One such preliminary wedge is sometimes offered by the

patient's physical posture. A brilliant young man purred velvety charm in all patient-therapist interchange, and I was beginning to despair of ever really getting to work on his self-defeatism. Finally, I asked him to note the position of his head. Why was it that he characteristically cocked his head to the side during sessions? Why did he turn it slightly to the side, so that I could not fully see his face? Why was it that when he spoke of certain things the angle at which he turned away would increase? What meaning was there in these postural phenomena?

"Nothing!" he said. "Absolutely nothing!" And on he purred. But I had collected evidence. There *was* pattern to his posture; there was clear relationship between it and the content of his verbalization. I persevered; and one productive day he turned his head away less, and began a flood of vituperation which ended, for quite a while, all traces of pleasantness during therapeutic sessions, but which led to eventual considerable growth and maturation of creative potentials.

The turning of the head, it developed, was the one small way his unconscious hatred of me found clearly identifiable expression. In shielding his face from my eyes, he could act out his distrust and defiance, albeit in small measure. But when this small spigot could no longer be employed with immunity from self-detection, the flood of resentment poured through to awareness. "I'm perfectly furious with you," he came eventually to say. "Sometimes I think you are running a great risk in having your head fastened to your shoulders by mere flesh. . . . I had the urge to knock your head off!" Thus, the purring ended. Therapeutic sessions became "unpleasant" indeed —but productive! For the first time in his life, the patient became aware of *what* he characteristically did in life; he became aware of *how* he operated in life.

Self-defeatism comprises much of the "what" in such operations. Its various forms within the clinic setting are noted; and then we ask: "What are you doing in your relations with people *outside* the office? What are you doing outside which corresponds to the self-defeatism we have noted here?"

For example, an extremely gifted man made of each session a very pleasant social exchange. It was truly delightful to hear of literature and politics, session after session. I found myself looking forward to each session with this person. They provided such relaxation from work. And that was, of course, their shortcoming: The man simply was not applying himself to the "fundamental rule" of therapy. He was not saying what came to mind, but was socializing charmingly and effectively. His behavior outside the clinic ran parallel. He was accepted everywhere as charming and desirable. People generally thought well of him, and considered him to be quite a "success." There was one difficulty. He did not think well of himself: He was actually a resounding failure. For he had lain down in life, exactly as he had in therapy. He was the perfect gentleman, the charming host, the debonair husband. But from the moment he arose in the morning to the time he closed his eyes at night, he virtually did not do a single thing which either really tapped his inner needs, or used the mainsprings of his inner life. His existence had become hollow formalism, exactly as his therapeutic sessions. He went through the motions of living, just as he pretended to free-associate at the clinic. To the superficial eye, his life was a solid success; and to the inadequately trained therapist, his behavior at the clinic would leave little to be desired. Actually, in both situations, he was passively rebelling against life—venting tremendous rage by turning it against his self-realization. Reasons for the gradual build-up of his tremendous rage against life were many. The build-up had been subtly gradual, and almost imperceptible. The man had come to the clinic with a localized loss of function in his right hand; but this localized dysfunction was only a small symbolic expression of the overpowering pressure toward ceasing to function, ceasing to serve, and ceasing to lend himself to exploitation.

Where the build-up of hostility is sufficiently intense, and where it is generally shielded from one's own awareness, it may—over a period of years—turn against one's own life and essentially undermine its basic validity. Such a life may become, as in this instance, hollow: a living protest against forces only inwardly perceived.

A first step is to recognize and perceive truly *what* is going on. Only later do we delve methodically into the *why* of it. We avoid premature preoccupation with the "why," for it is often a defense against truly accepting that the "what" of self-defeatism is actually occurring. Thus, the patient first becomes aware of his self-defeating tactics within the therapeutic situation, and only later does he experience the intense hatred which underlies it. It is difficult to convey with words the drama of the emerging fury which has been trapped for almost an entire lifetime. It is, for a while, quite irrational, surging forth like a mighty subterranean river and hurling itself at virtually all aspects of life. It is only later, after considerable adjustment to these underlying feelings, that the torrent is reduced to a calmer flow, and is directed into appropriate and constructive channels.

The recognition of secretiveness toward the therapist may lead to the discovery of unrealistic fears and anxieties. The withholding of information is often a clue to fears concerning the consequences of true communication. One woman who had that very day at work been awarded a complimentary title avoided telling me of her good fortune. And the question was raised as to what she feared, what caused the secretiveness. "What am I afraid of?" is at first a confounding question, for there are no obvious dangers in view. We take care, at such times, to refrain from reassuring the patient that he therefore *has* nothing to fear. Rather we encourage him to delve deep within his being for causes which *do* operate to produce anxiety, but whose precise natures are as yet unknown.

We deal in therapy with whatever grounds emerge, and often, as has been noted, in our culture these grounds relate to either emerging hostility or emerging sexual impulses. We have already explored many sources of anxiety; and of these, the one to which we pay most particular attention in work with self-defeatists is their anticipation of rejection over seeking to succeed, their anxiety associated with the impulse to achieve self-fulfillment.

Therapy cannot presume to eliminate fear. It only seeks to render such fears as are experienced more realistic. We endeavor to sharpen the perception of the realities of life, so that feelings and responses may be maximally appropriate both to the world within and to that without. For our faith is in the Biblical teaching—that truth does indeed serve human adjustment and long term happiness.

The grounds for anxiety are reached by devious paths. The woman under discussion reported: "I saw a girl on the train today who did something peculiar with her hair —and I became immensely frightened—as if someone had pointed a knife at me!" Analysis revealed that her mother had often displayed the same peculiar mannerism; that, due to therapy, the patient was now prone to experiencing her fear of authority figures more fully; and that coming face to face with this parent-related mannerism at this particular time unleashed a flood of parent-associated anxiety—a feeling which she had somehow held in check through the years.

Our work is conditioned by this understanding: Lack of success in life—underachievement regarding the dimensions of evolving selfhood—is not generally due to the absence of suitable reaction tendencies; and it is not due chiefly to *not knowing* what to do. It is due more essentially to inner conflict, to forces which oppose and combat implications of existing knowledge and existing suitable patterns of response; and one variety of force which conflicts with the urge to realize oneself is anxiety over success. Our therapeutic goals, therefore, involve the analysis of such anxiety.

This woman is helped to perceive, therefore, the workings of her anxiety over succeeding. She repeatedly examines the manifestations of this anxiety, and the forms taken by her defenses against feeling it, defenses which are injurious to her self-realization. Gradually, as these defenses are weakened, she comes to feel the underlying anxiety, and to experience it in direct connection with the urge to achieve a greater measure of self-fulfillment. With repetition, therefore, the associative bonds between anxiety and constructive effort are loosened and weakened. Such deconditioning of anxiety follows the usual laws of learning. As the patient bares her hopes for self-fulfillment in the presence of the new authority figure (the therapist), the old anticipation of rejection for such expressions is gradually extinguished. For the therapist does not condemn, but rather welcomes measures which validly court such fulfillment.

This process is similar to the deconditioning reported by the psychologist Mary C. Jones,[2] in which a child's fear of rabbits was extinguished through gradual exposure to a rabbit under conditions of safety. The child was, at first, extremely fearful; but—day by day, as the rabbit was brought closer, while the child played with well-adjusted children and ate favorite foods—the rabbit gradually became associated with pleasantness and security, rather than their reverse; and in the end, the child developed an actual fondness for rabbits. Moreover, these changes had transfer effect, for the child also became considerably less afraid of other varieties of strange animals, and developed an increased tolerance for strange things and unfamiliar situations.

The anxiety-creativity tie is thus gradually loosened. Moreover, the patient learns, through repeated interaction with the therapist, that self-defeat is not required for acceptance. The family constellation, in childhood, had required self-defeatism as a security operation; self-inflicted defeat had actually made for some semblance of emotional security during those threatening developmental years; but the patient now learns that self-defeat is not necessary for survival, that far more emotional security may ensue through abandoning the self-defeating pattern than was ever achieved by it. He learns this from the therapist's genuine professional dedication, and from the steadfastly constructive reception given to creative plans and activities.

Therapy deals also with unrealistic guilt: The phenomena of self-defeat set the stage for the discovery of inner self-condemnation. But these phenomena of self-defeat, as well as other varieties of phenomena manifesting guilt, are difficult to perceive, since again, defenses against recognizing the inner meaning of such occurrences have been in operation for many years. However, various oblique clues—such as a peculiar "anticipation of failure," as one person reported it, "as if something inside says 'You're going to fail anyway!' "—lead the stream of associations to *why* it is that one anticipates failure, and thus to a gradual growing awareness of feelings of guilt. Moreover, as one becomes more aware of long-buried hostilities, one also tends to feel more acutely the sense of culpability, the sense of guilt. One gradually comes to perceive manifestations of guilt in interpersonal relations. The sort of employment one keeps, the sort of employer one works for: These often reflect the quota of suffering, and the ways in which it is filled.

One woman, for example, who had become habituated to long and unnecessary conversations with a sadistic employer, became gradually aware of how inwardly bruised and humiliated she felt after each such exchange. Regardless of the subject discussed on any particular day, each conversation really centered around a single point: that the employer was a person of enormous worth, and that she was worthless. With increased awareness, she gradually shortened these conversational trips to the "whipping post," remarking one day with a wry smile that she felt considerably less tense and depressed after a day's work, but not so, apparently, her employer: "He prefers me the way I *was!*" The change had come about through discovering the inner meaning of her self-abusive behavior, uncovering the unrealistic grounds of her guilt, and working through and changing these grounds. The guilt over harboring hostility toward the parent and parent surrogates, over desiring self-determination, over setting one's own proper wishes and prerogatives before the parent's neurotic demands, are repeatedly aired in a new context. The self-hatred, the feelings of worthlessness—as one patient phrased it, "...the feeling that I am such a terrible person, that I simply do not deserve anything for

myself"—are subjected to extinction and counterconditioning.

Therapy itself arouses guilt feelings, for it represents
an effort at self-will, self-improvement; the unhealthy conscience which opposes such maturation therefore takes a
stand against this treatment. Such guilt feelings, as Freud
and others have advanced, weigh heavily against progress
in treatment. The patient becomes aware of the primi-
tively vicious and supposedly omnipotent nature of his
authoritarian conscience. For these qualities are projected
upon the therapist, and the patient will accordingly fear
the therapist at times, as if he possessed unlimited powers,
a godlike omniscience, and an unbridled egotism. These
qualities will then be viewed in sharp contrast, since the
therapist's warm concern, permissiveness, non-punitive
attitudes, apparent human limitations, and positive orientation toward the patient's expression of will and self-determination, all attest to significant distortion in the patient's
perception.

The authoritarian conscience is gradually changed. This
conscience came into being through introjection of a parental image; it is changed through being "extrojected"
upon the person of the therapist, as Mowrer phrased it.
Since such parental "clothing" should fit the therapist
badly, the need for re-tailoring one's inner conception of
authority—one's conscience—is continually before the
patient, and provides measurements for altering this conscience. "Therapy thus provides a kind of second childhood," continues Mowrer, "and a second chance at the
'unfinished business' of growing up." It renders the conscience more tolerant and benign, more accepting of creative will, less neurotically corruptible, i.e., less prone to
being bribed by unnecessary suffering. This second child-

hood is a variety of temporary regression, during which the patient remains for a while at a lower level of personality organization, meets conflicts and issues to which he had adjusted poorly during his development years, and gradually arrives at more wholesome solutions.

The self-defeatist's neurotic craving for power is discovered. This need is quite certain to manifest itself in the transference relationship, although the intent is likely to be veiled. We have already considered various pathological ways by which patients seek to be powerful in therapy, the many demands and reluctances through which they seek unconsciously to control therapy and the therapist. As therapy progresses, as changes occur and anxieties rise to the surface, the patient is likely to struggle even more rigidly to defend himself through power by maintaining control over all things in his life space. The recognition and analysis of this unrealistic craving for power—this control of therapy—is essential for a basic, salutary personality reorganization. We look beneath the need for power, peer beyond the neurotic hostility. We examine the anxiety and depression which are circumvented by the power defense or the inappropriate hostility. We must deal with the unrealistic generators of anxiety, and dissolve related threats to the sense of personal significance. For unless these deeper causes are alleviated, personality reorganization will fall short of being optimally self-sustaining.

In an atmosphere of honest professional dedication, in which the self-defeatist's unconscious deceitfulness is gradually displaced by an increasing respect for truth, there dawns an understanding of the terrible price exacted by habitual power operations. The hollowness of the victories won by controlling and primitive omnipotence seeking, the futility of perfectionistic strivings, the self-defeat in resis-

tance offered to the processes of therapy: these seep gradually into awareness, and set the stage for the emergence
of change.

THE EMERGENCE OF CHANGE

The self-defeatist comes to perceive pattern in his life.
Occurrences are now less a series of isolated events, since
expanded awareness relates these events, and perceives
meaning in them. There emerges a sense of continuity in
life, a comprehension of one's present self as a logical
consequence of the past. The present personality organization, the nature of operating defenses, and the chronic
distortions in perception—all find due parentage in the
trials of former experience. The role of blind obedience
is lessened and the role of reason in the governing of life
is increased; one's creative urge is conditioned less by the
fancied world of yesteryear and more by the real world
of today; one's dependency upon others assumes more
realistic dimensions, and sheds the "matter of life or death"
necessity of childhood.

One emerges from the little world of childhood, where
life has meaning—almost entirely—in relation to the parent.
A man who had been wrapped up in this little world, who
had so unremittingly and subtly defied his parent at every
turn as to have little energy left for self-realization, finally
began to extricate himself, and realized: "I have become
aware of how unrelated to my real wants in life are my
actual daily activities." And later, he decided upon a
change of occupation, a change which might satisfy his
own valid needs, rather than function primarily as a cause
of dissatisfaction to his parent.

Expanding awareness takes the place of dissociation,

and healthful mechanisms of control supplant extensive repression. The perception of one's life space grows and sharpens; one more fully experiences both the outer world of events, and the inner world of feeling. One develops the attitude of perceiving oneself, of being an object to oneself, of utilizing the intelligence in order to view one's own activities and being, and to make continual changes in the light of such intelligence.

There emerges an increased awareness of resentment. The therapist is the catalyst. Such resentment is first transferred onto him, and through analysis of this transferred feeling, it is later directed into more appropriate channels. "I am becoming more aware of myself," a student associated. "I am becoming aware of what I am doing with my hostility. . . . I now see so *much* resentment— taking up so much of my existence. . . . And I wonder how I went through life without seeing it before! . . . How did I defend myself against seeing it?"

Once hostility is exposed to reason it is gradually directed by that reason. The recognition of self-destructive modes of venting resentment tends toward the creation of more wholesome patterns of discharge as substitutes. The woman who recognizes that when she is resentful toward the world she lies down, so to speak, and lets herself be trampled upon—feeling "They'll be sorry for what they do to me!"—tends to employ this masochistic pattern less and less. The man who comes to appreciate that his overt pugnacity actually harms himself more than it defends, learns to extend the periods of calm between self-destructive outbursts. The acceptance of one's hostility and the gradual directing of it along realistic channels relieve the inner pressure of subterranean resentment, and increasingly permit the acceptance of further resentment—the seeing of oneself as irritated and angry

—without immediately and rigidly condemning oneself categorically.

The ego ideal changes. One is content to be resentful *provided* that the feeling is realistic and just. One may now face the world of reality—both inner and outer—without being overwhelmed by feelings of "badness" and insignificance. For frustrations are bound to be met, and resentments to be engendered by them. Abiding peace is therefore possible only to the individual who can accept the naturalness of such hostilities, who insists only upon their change by reason. This acceptance of hostility permits a reaction to the world with markedly less guilt. It permits a measured rebuttal to chronic disparagement, rather than the former habit of immature temper outbursts—a response which brought humiliation and a further guilt. It therefore permits a gradual diminution of the grounds of guilt. Thus, by relieving the pressure of guilt, it helps create that psychological distance which is of assistance in the process of confronting the overly severe authoritarian conscience.

Therapy which assists self-realization generally involves a transition from an overemphasis on defense through individual power, toward defense through love and mutualism. This has been stated by the masters in a variety of ways: Karl Abraham formulated this personality movement in terms of overcoming "narcissistic reserve" and bringing about a "positive transference"; Alfred Adler described a similar transition as increasing the individual's "social feeling" and "communal consciousness."

With increasing inner orientation toward mutualism and the common good, and with an increasingly constructive directing of hostility, the guilt associated with exercising one's will clearly declines. The patient is increasingly able to accept his will in action, to affirm his self-directed separateness, to justify his nature to his conscience. Therapy involves exercises in the actual function of creative will. Such exercises take place in the presence of a figure of authority (the therapist). The presence may be actual—as during the sessions themselves—or psychological—as between sessions—for the patient will report major plans and efforts. Accordingly, these exercises in will function occur within a microcosm containing all the essentials of the will-guilt problem, and therefore involve and permit the working through of the implications of guilt concerning self-expression. During such exercises one man said: "My expression of will is like a child learning to walk. I feel anxious and insecure as I try. . . . But I feel myself becoming less so."

There is consequently an increasing freedom to employ the intelligence in one's own best interests, to be intelligent *for oneself;* to persevere constructively, and turn from self-destructive expedients; to replace dominance by a tyrannical authoritarian conscience with a self-directed creative purpose; to disengage oneself from the waste of time and energy in fighting over yesterday's hurts and disappointments; to live more validly in today's realities; to possess more complete accessibility to the rich reservoir of the unconscious—more abundant associations, higher energy level—as inhibitions are worked through; and finally, to reach a better integrated and more mature level of personality organization.

Strangely enough, it often comes as a surprising revelation to self-defeatists that creative effort may be pursued for advantage to self, rather than for simply continuing a drawn out struggle with the ubiquitous authority figure. One man at this stage reported: "This morning, for the first time, I had the feeling that the commissions I would make—I would make for *myself*! I had always known this intellectually; but this morning, for the first time, I *felt* I was working for myself."

There is a gradual change in the inner meaning of purposeful effort *away* from disservice to another, and *toward* service to oneself. Accordingly, the anxiety and guilt formerly attached to such effort are attenuated. There subsequently emerges a more positive conception of self. One is better able to tolerate good fortune—even to enjoy it—without being overwhelmed by guilt.

A keen desire for power remains; but it is a desire for realistic capability and independence, oriented toward adult accomplishment, rather than childhood's magical omnipotence. It is more realistically practical, rather than self-defeatingly perfectionistic, and is harnessed to broad and good purpose, rather than to neurotic revenge. It tends more toward a conquest of inanimate nature and the world of ideas and forces than toward the control or exploitation of other living things.

Through therapy, a freeing of spontaneous creative expression tends to emerge. And while we are not always successful in treatment, our successes are frequent enough, and of sufficient degree, to affirm our faith in this method of assisting people to increased creative fulfillment. Our faith is reinforced by the rationale of our method: that man's own reason can lead to understanding, and understanding to wisdom.

For reason is the lamp of life. And psychotherapy, at its best, is but a modern refinement of ancient practices whereby contemplation and counsel are blended in a process which enhances the effectiveness of every man's own inner light, that he may better read the signs of his unique larger existence, and better find the paths toward the realization of what he most values in his potential self.

NOTES

[1] Technical approaches to the subject matter of this chapter will be found in my article "The Problem of the Defeating Patient in Psychotherapy," *American Journal of Psychotherapy*, Vol. 8 (1954), pp. 703–718, and in Chapter 8 of *The Urge to Mass Destruction*, "Changing the Pattern of Self-and-Other Defeat: Psychotherapy." In these two prior treatments I have presented a systematic and documented review of the literature in this area, including genetic, dynamic, operational, and technical elements; and I have offered a rationale for comprehending various posited—and sometimes divergent—points of view.

[2] Mary C. Jones, "A Laboratory Study of Fear: The Case of Peter" in *Pedagogical Seminary*, Vol. 31 (1924), pp. 308–315.